THE BIG PICTURE

JEVON CALDWELL-GROSS
NICOLE CALDWELL-GROSS

THE BIG PICTURE

SEEING GOD'S DREAM FOR YOUR LIFE

....

Abingdon Press / Nashville

THE BIG PICTURE

SEEING GOD'S DREAM FOR YOUR LIFE

Library of Congress Control Number: 2022935213

978-1-7910-2595-3

MANUFACTURED IN THE UNITED STATES OF AMERICA

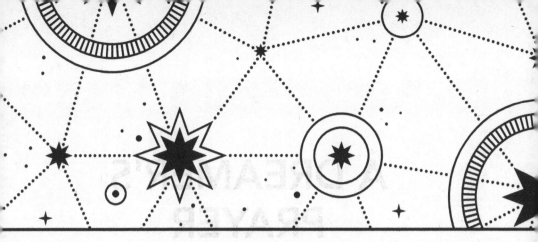

CONTENTS

A DREAMER'S PRAYER

God, I want your dream for my life.

Nothing smaller.

Nothing limited.

Nothing inherited.

Nothing compared.

Nothing muted.

Your big, expansive dream.

Impossible for me to see without you.

Impossible for me to do without you.

Impossible for me to be without you.

Let me dream.

Let me dream.

Let me dream, again.

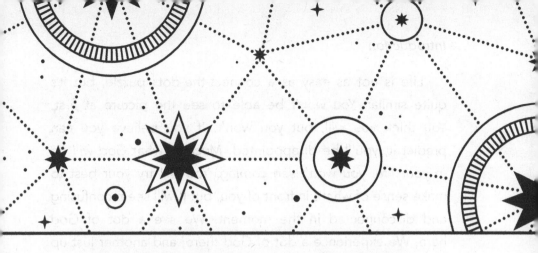

INTRODUCTION

Our daughter Olivia looked intently, but still couldn't see it. Here was yet another homework assignment designed to increase her love for counting. The sheet was covered with small dots and corresponding numbers. To a young mind that was still learning to count to one hundred, the dots seemed so random. She stared hopelessly at the page trying to identify the image, with no luck. The first attempt at connecting the dots by random plotting proved unsuccessful. We could always see the image, but she couldn't. Frustration grew. Confidence lowered. We had to reread the directions. When cooler heads prevailed, Olivia started with the number 1 and began connecting the dots, one by one. Slowly but surely, the pencil made the connections to the ascending numbers and a picture started to emerge. I could see it, but she had to finish the process to recognize it. After the last dot was connected, a familiar image was now visible. Frustration lowered. Confidence increased. Then the coloring commenced after a verbal affirmation of our child's own work. The dots were not so random after all.

Introduction

Life is not as easy as a connect-the-dots puzzle, but it's quite similar. You won't be able to see the picture at first. You think you will, but you won't. If you believe you can predict it, you'll be disappointed. *Much of what God will do in your life, you won't see coming.* You will try your best to make sense of what's in front of you, but it will seem confusing and disconnected in the moment. We see a dot of God here. We experience a dot of God there, and another just up ahead, but we aren't sure how it all connects or if it connects at all. The picture will be hard to decipher. It will look like a random scattering of dots. We encounter familiar feelings of frustration. It leaves us trying to connect and make sense out of seemingly disjointed moments. What was the purpose behind this setback? Why did God bring this person into my life? Why did God let them leave? What is God trying to show me? The people we meet will appear random, the decisions pointless, and the places insignificant. You won't see the big picture.

Søren Kierkegaard once said, "Life can only be understood backwards; but it must be lived forwards." This is an affirmation of our willingness to reflect on the past, but it's also a confession of the things we miss in the moment. It's an acknowledgment of our inability to truly understand the present. We forge ahead, pushing through our joys and sorrows. However, most of us can agree that many of the lessons and transformative experiences we have are understood only in hindsight. We see the value—after the fact. This is especially true when our experiences are painful or difficult. We thank God for those instances when we can file them away as things of the past. We embrace the lessons learned when they are finally in our rearview mirror. But let's be honest: they don't feel like that in the moment. The lessons feel like punishments. What we now call a blessing once felt like a curse. The source of today's joy was a previous thorn in our side. It's difficult to see or even recognize the value of God's movement in our lives in the present.

Another writer describes it in this manner:

> "When things go unnoticed for too long, bad things begin to happen. A leaky roof turns into a major repair of an entire wall; unattended weeds eventually squelch the growth of the vegetables; a 'not that big-a-deal' lump over time becomes cancerous; an undisciplined child later in life lacks a healthy sense of boundary....Time has a way of forcing things to get the attention they need. Many in our culture have lived with a sense of 'unnoticedness' for too long. And it's time for us to take notice."[1]

This book is an invitation to take notice. It's a journey of discovering and rediscovering the presence of God in our lives. It's an invitation into the continual process of connecting the seemingly random moments that may have gone unnoticed or overlooked. It's courageously looking back in order to look forward. When we start connecting the dots, we see not only a God that has been present, but a God that is still very much active in our lives today. Because it's only when the dots start to connect that we see beyond the moment, beyond this season, and begin to see "the Big Picture." It's here that frustration decreases and confidence increases. This will be important on our journey together, for this reason: most of what God will do in your life you won't see coming. You think you will, but you won't.

CHAPTER 1
I CAN'T SEE IT

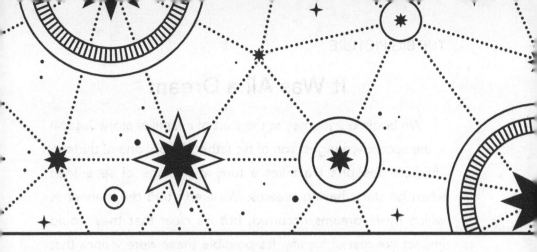

CHAPTER 1
I CAN'T SEE IT
Jevon

Joseph had a dream and told it to his brothers, which made them hate him even more. He said to them, "Listen to this dream I had. When we were binding stalks of grain in the field, my stalk got up and stood upright, while your stalks gathered around it and bowed down to my stalk."

His brothers said to him, "Will you really be our king and rule over us?" So they hated him even more because of the dreams he told them.

Then Joseph had another dream and described it to his brothers: "I've just dreamed again, and this time the sun and the moon and eleven stars were bowing down to me."

When he described it to his father and brothers, his father scolded him and said to him, "What kind of dreams have you dreamed? Am I and your mother and your brothers supposed to come and bow down to the ground in front of you?" His brothers were jealous of him, but his father took careful note of the matter.

(Genesis 37:5-11)

It Was All a Dream

We begin our journey at the start of a familiar story. Joseph is the second-youngest son of his father, Jacob; one of thirteen children. Joseph's life takes a turn at the age of seventeen when he starts having dreams. We aren't told the manner in which these dreams occurred, but it's clear that they would impact the rest of his life. It's possible these were visions that came to him in the middle of the night while he was sound asleep. Or maybe he was going about his daily work in the fields and started daydreaming during his down time. The how really didn't matter to Joseph, nor should it for us. He had the dreams. And when dreams come, things won't be the same.

In his first dream, Joseph envisions that he is out in the fields bundling grain and something unexpected happens. The grain has a mind of its own. His bundle stands upright and the bundles belonging to his brothers start bowing down to his (Genesis 37:6-7). His second dream is similar, but with imagery that seems to be more confusing than the first. This time, he sees the sun, moon, and eleven stars bowing at his feet (37:9).

What does it all mean? Bundles of grain don't stand or bow by themselves. The sun, moon, and stars don't bow before anything. The imagery of his dreams, and its implication, raises a host of questions. Where did these dreams originate? Were they just figments of his imagination? Were they just wishful thinking? Could they be messages from God? Are they something Joseph's subconscious mind created out of spite? Why this? Why now? What was God up to?

The dots don't connect. Joseph can't see it. He doesn't understand it. Sounds absurd, doesn't it?

Joseph was a dreamer born into an average family with average problems in the middle of nowhere, surrounded by average people. There is no compelling evidence that Joseph was overly ambitious or obsessed with visions of grandeur. He was favored by his father, but he did not have a history of chasing after power and status. Yet, every day, while Jacob's sons were laboring in the fields, someone with big dreams existed in their midst.

We walk past them every day. We sit next to them at coffee shops. We stand in line behind them at the grocery stores. You work with them. You sit next to them in the pews in church. We may even see them when we look in the mirror. They aren't always loud. They don't always post their ideas on social media or spend time perfecting their vision boards. Sometimes they don't look like dreamers. But they are ordinary people who are open to receiving a word and vision from God. They don't see it, at least not all of it, right away. We don't see it. Joseph didn't see it. The dots were not lining up. Joseph never saw this coming.

Alternatives We Have Never Considered

I love repeats and reruns. I spend most of my time watching shows that have already aired. Nicole and I have watched every spin-off of *Law and Order* imaginable. It feels like I personally know Captain Benson and Detective Stabler, and Jack McCoy has been a topic of conversation on several occasions. The show *Martin* is and will always be a classic. I can recite every line spoken by the security guard Otis, and act out every scene by Dragon Fly Jones. I will stand on my belief that

A Different World never gets old. There is something comfortable and familiar about reruns. The endings are predictable. The characters are familiar. I can't be the only one who loves reruns, because some of these actors still get paid an exorbitant amount of money from syndication as their shows continue to air year after year.

Joseph's life was destined to play out like a rerun. It was stuck on repeat. He had been trained to continue the family business as planned. The area where their father had settled would be the place where he would live out the rest of his days. There were ten older brothers, and each one lived the same episode. Except for the firstborn, they all had similar expectations for their lives. They would watch their father's flocks, grow their herds, get married, have children, and continue the story. Joseph got a chance to watch ten seasons of this show. Doing something different was neither encouraged nor readily available. His options were anything but plentiful. On the surface, there were no variations to this predictable ending. His life was going to be a rerun—good, familiar, but not unpredictable. So he thought.

So we often think. As the days continue to pass by in our lives, we become locked into a routine. There are times we find comfort in the rhythm. It's what we know. It's what we have mastered. We know the characters. We know the endings. There are few surprises. That is, until God shows us that something different is possible.

When Joseph started dreaming, it was God's way of showing him a new future. God showed him that a different life was possible. That mere glimpse inside of the unimaginable exposes him to a world of possibilities. It allows Joseph—and us—to reconsider and reimagine what we once thought was fixed and no longer up for negotiation. *Before the dream gives clarity, it provides what many people think is lost: options.* The dreams get Joseph's mind turning and upend what he took for granted. The images and pictures in his mind start to expand. What else is possible that he has yet to consider? The future we imagined in our minds starts to crumble, and that which we pictured starts to take a different shape. We have options we'd never previously considered. This is what happens when a person gets exposed to another way of using their gifts that they have never considered. It's what happens when someone changes their profession later in life. It's the person who grows up in a troubled family and then realizes that this doesn't have to be their story too. It's the individual who thought their life was headed in a certain direction, but sees something, hears something, and gets exposed to an outcome that they never thought was possible. It's seeing someone with a similar background in a particular role that opens one's eyes to the possibilities. It can be one of the most freeing and redemptive moments along our faith journey. One of the most impactful pictures that God can show us is when God reminds us that something different is possible.

One of the most impactful pictures that God can show us is when God reminds us that something different is possible.

The freedom of the dream brings challenges that we must welcome. When you've been exposed to this new world of possibilities, it's hard to see life through the same vantage point. The fields that Joseph visited every day for the past seventeen years suddenly take on a new meaning. The office where we work doesn't look the same. Certain friendships are reevaluated. Joseph can no longer gather grain in the same manner as he did before the grand vision. While everyone else is working, I can imagine him daydreaming about the bundles standing up and bowing down. Every time the sun and moon rise and set, Joseph is reminded of what's possible.

Most importantly, he sees himself differently. He is not just another son in a long line of siblings. Could it be that God has a different future for him? While he can't understand or comprehend the meaning of this dream, it gives him a picture of himself that he's never considered. Are we ready for a dream that not only challenges our plans, but who God wants us to become? The dream changes our future, but in the process it changes us. It shows us a version of ourselves that we didn't think was possible. It forces us to reevaluate the narrow version of self that we've always imagined.

This is as challenging as it is inspirational. Rarely does God intervene in our lives to give us a picture of what we have already seen or accomplished. The nature of its arrival signals that something different is at hand. This will be hard for many to embrace. Even the images and ideas that we conjure in our minds are limiting. When we close our eyes, our minds drift to familiar possibilities. The pictures and images that form are often based on past experiences. It happens to the best of us, even down to the smallest detail. The people we see are familiar faces. The places are the ones that are known. Even the outcomes are predictable. We love our repeats. We think about the money and the resources that we have available. The picture that we see is filtered through our background, our résumé, our failures, and our connections. If we aren't careful, the image brought to mind by the dream simply becomes a glorified rerun. However, that is not what God wants to do in our lives. God did not mysteriously intervene in the life of Joseph to give him a picture that he had already seen. The presence of God in our lives is not a call to simply repeat the things we have already accomplished. It challenges the very notion of what we deem to be possible. The dream might not resemble anything you've seen or have previously experienced. It's hard to see what we have never considered to be a possibility.

A Dream with No Details

Many readers accuse Joseph of being arrogant and without tact as he shares his dreams with his brothers. Thanks to their father's favoritism, Joseph's brothers already hate him. Now he seems to rub his dreams in the faces of the very people who despised him. Joseph is often portrayed as a petty sibling with a vendetta to settle. Is it possible that he's making an already complicated relationship worse? Absolutely. He is not the favorite on his brothers' lists. Is it possible that sharing his dream will cause even more tension? Possibly.

But isn't it also possible that Joseph is just looking for somebody to help him connect the dots? Isn't it just as likely that he doesn't comprehend his own dreams, and he's looking for someone who knows him to help him make sense of the things that he's seen?

Remember, Joseph was only seventeen years old when he started having these dreams. I don't know what you were like at seventeen, but I don't think I was mature enough to understand every move that God was making in my life. I didn't then, and

I still don't. Perhaps Joseph is coming to his brothers with his dreams because he's looking for answers. He is searching for an explanation for the meaning of these dreams and visions. He is searching for clarity. He's seeking understanding.

Isn't this a familiar search? At the core of what we desire is finding the answers to what we can't understand. We couldn't see what purpose a particular obstacle served, so we searched for answers. We couldn't see why this person came into our lives. We didn't know why they left. We couldn't see how something promised was going to unfold. Much of what we desire from God are answers to the unanswered questions about life.

We have even become proficient at trying to coerce the answers when we reach a point of desperation. We surrender ourselves to spiritual disciplines designed to get the attention of God. We fast. We pray. We plan a revival. We engage in this or that spiritual practice in hopes of finding the right answers that we believe are hidden in a divine vault. While I don't doubt the power of intentionally seeking after God, I'm not certain it's always so simple and formulaic.

One of the biggest misconceptions about faith is that it gives us all the answers. Here is the real, unadulterated truth: an honest walk with God will lend you more questions than answers. It will yield more mystery. It will unearth more uncertainty than what existed previously. The pastor of Change Church, Dharius Daniels, refers to these moments as "seasons of ambiguity." These are periods in our lives where the purpose or moves of God are veiled. We aren't sure of the next steps. The present is confusing, and the future appears uncertain. There is no escaping the hard truth that every faith journey comes with seasons of ambiguity. The picture isn't clear.

An honest walk with God will lend you more questions than answers.

And yet, there is one promise God does not make. God never promises our complete understanding. God gives us a lot of assurance. God promises us that God will never leave us or forsake us. God promises us that our needs will be met according to God's riches and glory. God promises unconditional love, presence, power, forgiveness, and even life beyond the grave. Yet of all the promises that we find within the Bible, there is not one that hints at God's commitment for us to always understand or have absolute clarity.

Many people give up on faith, disconnect from God, or lose faith in themselves because when they were looking for answers, it seemed like all they received was ambiguity. They didn't abandon their search for answers; they just committed to finding them through other means. Can we really trust God when we have more questions than answers?

And yet, questions without answers, or at least without easy answers, seems to be a pattern with God. God consistently operates in ambiguity. Think about how much ambiguity is surrounding Joseph's dreams. Joseph's brothers will bow down to him. That's it, and even that is open to interpretation. In the dreams, it's the bundles of grain and heavenly bodies that bow. It seems like these represent the brothers, but does Joseph know that for sure? And even if he accepts that, there's no indication of how or when it will come about. God gives Joseph a dream with no details! There was no commentary. No fine print. No explanations or interpretations. The dreams brought more questions than clarity. God gave Joseph just enough to stir the pot, but not enough to clear the air. It is just enough to instill hope but not enough to decrease anxiety. This is a difficult dream to embrace without much detail. God could have easily explained to Joseph why this was going to happen, when it was going to unfold. God could have reassured him with an outline showing how all the dots would connect. However, God does not fill in the gaps. God does not offer any helpful information to lower Joseph's anxiety.

At least God is consistent! This is exactly how God acts when instructing Abraham and Sarah to seek out the promised land. God approaches an elderly couple in their seasoned years with the promise of a family and new real estate, only describing it as "the land that I will show you" (Genesis 12:1). In Exodus, the Israelites are told they would be freed from Egypt and taken to "a land full of milk and honey" (3:17). God leaves out the detail that this will require them to fight the toughest battles of their lives. God tells David, a teenager, that he was next in line to be king. Again, God conveniently leaves out the loss of a best friend and the betrayal of a mentor. Jesus tells a group of fishermen, "Come, follow me...and I'll show you how to fish for people" (Matthew 4:19). He casually leaves out that they will have to fend for their lives. God is never short on dreams but frequently short on details. It's as though we are on a need-to-know basis with God.

Maybe God leaves the dots unconnected for a reason. One reason why we only get glimpses, a dot here and a dot there, is because if God connects the dots too early, there are many experiences that might lead us to prematurely abandon our dreams and our callings. Imagine if God was honest with Joseph about the road ahead. Joseph's dreams would be fulfilled after he endured years of slavery and imprisonment, after being sold by his own brothers. How do you think Joseph would respond if God mentioned the pits and prisons from the outset? Our faith is barely strong enough to believe the dream, let alone withstand the accompanying details. Many of us would walk away from the very things we have been praying for if we knew all that they entailed. If you saw the complete picture, you might not be able to handle it! Every dream comes with hidden details that are necessary and yet hard to comprehend.

If we really knew how hard relationships really were, would we even give them a chance? Imagine if we were fully aware at the beginning of the difficulties of starting a business, going back to school, starting a new job, dating again, moving again, or joining a church. The road to get there might be too intimidating. The details can be daunting. They can overshadow the possibilities. It's tempting to focus on details and lose sight of God's bigger picture for our lives. The struggles might be overwhelming. If we were aware of every detail, we might have abandoned some of the best things that have ever happened to us.

The ambiguity of our dreams is not meant to confuse, but to protect. God gives us what we can digest in that moment. God loves us enough to give us the amount of information that we can comprehend and act on. The ambiguity and uncertainty in our dreams are not a matter of God's punishment. They are not a sign that we are moving in the wrong direction. And they are certainly not proof that the dream was a sham. *Ambiguity is a decision by a loving God to reveal what our minds can digest without being overwhelmed.*

This suggests that there will be seasons in your life where you will have to keep moving in the presence of ambiguity. Joseph's life could not wait for clarity. Moving during this time requires a commitment to keep showing up to the places where God has positioned us without knowing how it all connects. It takes the daily practicing of parenting, working, learning, schooling, growing, evolving—not because their meaning is clear, but because it's what we are called to do for this season of our lives.

Unpredictable

There was nothing in Joseph's life that connected to God's bigger picture. There was no present indicator that hinted to the future reality that his dreams revealed. No dot or experience signaled a rise in power or authority for Joseph. There was nothing that indicated the likelihood of people kneeling at his feet. From what we know, Joseph was not part of an internship program that intentionally develops young leaders for future success. There are no discussions around changing the expectations around heirs and birthrights. There has been absolutely no talk about relocating to different lands.

When we perform an inventory of our gifts, we look for signs that we have the skills and abilities necessary to bring our dreams to reality. We are tempted to look for some indication that we have what it takes. If Joseph did this, what would he have seen? I imagine he would have looked around at his experiences and wondered how the present would connect to the bigger picture. How would being one of the youngest, working out in the fields, have led to his family bowing at his feet? God showed Joseph what appeared to be a place of prominence.

The only problem was that there was no path that he could imagine that could take him from his current responsibilities to seeing his dream come to fruition. It's hard for him to truly embrace what he sees because there is no straight line from being out in the fields to having people bow at his feet. That gap between the dots is too great. The present and the picture of the future do not connect.

This is often where faith is lost, and the big picture is questioned. It's in between the dots. When we surrender to the idea, we cannot predict, manipulate, or control how the dots connect. The dots seem as they are—on opposite ends of the page with no points or places of connection. It happens to the best of us. God gives us a glimpse of a bigger picture that reignites our faith. It helps us to uncover passions and dreams that did not previously exist, or that we thought we'd left behind. So, we start searching for indicators. We carefully study the dots in our past. We reflect on the transformative moments in our present. Then we hopefully look at those things that are yet to come and desperately try to discern how they relate. We attempt to draw these neatly ordered lines between our present and the picture of our past. As best we can, we try to chart the course based on the dots that we see.

This is where trust is needed. There are moments in our faith journey when we won't be able to draw a straight line from where we are to where God needs us to be. *Faith is not lived in straight lines.* The dream is not predicated on our ability to know how it will connect. It is frustrating because we are trying to connect the dots we see today as if those are the only available ones for God to use. If it was a picture of future companionship, we would try to draw a straight line from all the viable candidates we currently know. (This can be quite depressing.)

We anxiously check the current job openings. We stalk the housing markets. We take inventory of all of our connections to determine which of these might open the right door. Our minds run countless scenarios depicting the connections and possibilities. We obsessively look for a viable path that will help bridge the present to God's picture. Similar to Joseph, we realize that none of it makes sense. There is not a direct path. When they don't connect, doubt finds its way into the dream.

The way forward is to trust that God can take what seems totally unconnected, disjointed, or random and find some way for the dream to unfold. There is often so much contradiction in what God shows us and what we see with our own eyes. And yet, it is in the gap that we have to trust that God can connect two contradictory experiences and somehow make them fit. It's embracing a bigger picture even when the dots are not connecting. It's how inexperienced people in the Bible became viable candidates over the more experienced. It's seen in how people with scarred pasts and public failures were expected to do great things. It's how God would ultimately work outside of cultural boundaries, religious expectations, and gender limitations to bring about change. It's when our belief does not waver, even when you see the gaps increase. It's trusting that God can take what appears to be direct contradictions and somehow make them relate.

They Can't See It

Everyone had an opinion about God's dream for Joseph's life. The challenge is not just his ability to embrace what he can't fully understand, but how he responds based on what he hears from others.

I can see Joseph posting his dreams online, anticipating the notifications of encouragement. He overcomes his nerves of going public and presses "post." He waits for the right time of day to ensure that as many people see his message as possible. Joseph hopes to see the "likes" and words of inspiration. He checks every few minutes to confirm how much the engagement numbers have increased. Maybe it was not the right time to post. Did they change the algorithm again? Perhaps he didn't use the right buzzwords. Maybe it's the wrong platform. Then the responses start to trickle in, and they aren't favorable. Angry emojis. Ridicule, disbelief, people listing all the reasons he can't do it or why he shouldn't.

It's hard when your dreams are met with discouragement. The disbelief hurts. The critics' words sting when they come alive. Questions are raised. Doubts are expressed. The "laughing emoji" is in full use.

The only answer Joseph received was a reminder of the ridiculous nature of this dream. His brothers were not convinced or impressed. I'm sure they reminded him of every reason why it wasn't possible. Listing the name of every older brother in line before him would have ended the discussion. Their culture determined power and authority by one's birth order. His dream would have been more believable if it maybe insinuated the death of his brothers and Joseph being the designated survivor. That would make for a better story line and discussion, but of course it wouldn't have made the brothers more receptive to it.

I've learned that there are some seasons where the prayer is not "God, help me to understand it," but instead "God, help me to deal with the responses when the dream becomes public." Some of us can handle the ambiguity, but the absurdity of the dream invites the solicited and unsolicited opinions of others. This is what gives us pause and raises second thoughts. It blurs the lines of connection and makes us doubt our glimpses of this bigger picture. God-given dreams will always be accompanied by an array of judgments. They will come from afar and from those who are close.

Joseph's brothers can't see it and are vocal about their disbelief. Joseph learns that proximity does not always yield the same perspective. It's fascinating because he sees them every day. They work together. They eat together. They travel together. They live together. One would logically assume that they would be able to "see" together. And yet, this does not change their perspective.

We see this in our own lives quite often. Many of you have wondered why the people in your home or your own family can have such different political perspectives. It has either been the cause of heavy disagreements or an agreed-upon off-limit topic. It shocks our system because the assumption is that people in close proximity should share the same perspective. But they don't. People we're close to can share different spending habits, express love differently, have different hobbies, and even hold different ideas about faith. Coworkers have different aspirations and ambitions. Even the best of friends can argue about their views on vaccinations and mask-wearing. People in close proximity can and will have vastly different dreams.

Joseph's brothers, the ones who hated him, could not see God's bigger picture. Imagine being one of his brothers. Their words and disbelief were directed at Joseph, but they say something about the brothers themselves. Disbelief was an admission of their limitations. Had they ever seen themselves bowing to Joseph? Probably not. Had they ever received a dream that they would be in a position of power? I'm not so sure. They never imagined they could live outside their cultural limitations. They could not see beyond their own faith or their birth order. They could not imagine life beyond the fields. If they couldn't see it for themselves, they certainly couldn't see it for Joseph. To affirm Joseph's dream would be to affirm that something different is possible. That was something they could not embrace. And it's hard for people to see in you what they have never seen for themselves.

Love and Belief

If there was anyone who could comfort him, it was Joseph's father. Jacob loved Joseph. His father was not ashamed to say it or show it. Everyone knew that Joseph was Jacob's favorite. He had the coat and the gifts to prove it—which contributed to the brothers' anger toward him. His father's love was something that Joseph never doubted. If anyone in that community could see and affirm what God was showing Joseph, it would be his father.

Not only could his father affirm him, he also could understand Joseph. His father's life was an example of living outside of cultural expectations. Maybe Jacob forgot this part of his story. Considering the details of his upbringing, Joseph's dreams shouldn't have seemed too far-fetched to Jacob.

Jacob was the younger of a set of twins and carried the family tradition of being favored by one of his parents. It was prophesied before their birth that the older would serve the younger (Genesis 25:23). As the two grew in age, the dots started to connect. Through lies and deceit, Jacob tricked his older brother Esau into relinquishing his birthright as the firstborn son. That was only the start of the downward spiral. As his father lay on his deathbed, Jacob and his mother devised another plot to steal the blessing that belonged to Esau (Genesis 27). For years, this tore the family apart. The inheritance should have been given to his older brother, Esau. The land they were currently living in should have been given to the older son, and with it, God's promise of descendants and blessing first given to Abraham. However, that's not how this story unfolds. While the details of Jacob's ascent are morally questionable, the reality is undeniable. Jacob is a living testament that none of us is bound by cultural limitations.

If there was any chance of someone seeing and understanding God's dream for Joseph, his father was his last hope. But even with a parent's favor and similar story of his own, Jacob couldn't see it either. It's a helpful reminder that everyone who loves you won't always believe in you.

Love and belief are not synonymous.

Love and belief are not synonymous. While love is often an expression of the heart, belief is an exercise of the mind. We make a grave mistake if we assume the two always work in tandem. While they can, they sometimes don't. Our hearts are broken, and our spirits are crushed when we desperately search for belief from the people who openly express their love. We question the validity of our dreams when the lack of support comes from unexpected places. We are even tempted to reevaluate the extent of their love. We can deal with the disbelief from jealous brothers, but few of us anticipate this response from places of love.

It hurts when disbelief comes from people whom we've known for years, people who know our secrets, and people who have celebrated key milestones in our lives. It hurts when those who know us best can't see it in us or for us. They are friends. They are spouses. They are mentors and coworkers. They are parents. They are teachers. They are loving people. They are caring people who can't see it. It almost seems contradictory. Have there been times in your life where disbelief came from unexpected places?

Love and belief are not synonymous. Those who love us may not always believe our dreams. But the opposite is also true. The absence of belief does not negate the presence of love. You will encounter individuals who love you but can't be the early adopters to the dreams that God has given to you. It means you can't remove everyone from your life who will not support every idea that you express. This does not give them a license to spread their disbelief. Nor does it give them permission to be an obstacle. It just leaves room for their belief to catch up to their love. Sometimes it's personal, and other times it's not. Remember, it's hard for people to see the possibilities beyond their own experience. They can't believe in you what they don't believe is possible in themselves. It could be that your dream pushes their faith to the point of disbelief. Perhaps they might believe in you if you come with a dream that fits the size of their faith. They would be encouraging if you shrunk the size of the dream to fit in a smaller box. Maybe if you had more details. Maybe if your dream depicted them in a better light.

And let's be honest, there are times when we are asking for people to have blind faith. Here's a hard question: "Have you done enough to earn people's belief?" People love us unconditionally, but belief is earned over time. It is the result of being committed to a particular behavior or outcome over time. I kept hearing this message in my reels online, and thought it appropriate to our response when we find ourselves dreaming alone:

> Here's the truth: This is the reality, okay. Nobody is going to believe in you until you've already done it. Nobody is going to come and celebrate with you until you've already done it. The work is going to come before the belief. Which means you're going to have to work for a long...time, by yourself, with no applause, with no awards, with nobody telling you good job.[2]

There are times when you might be the only one who believes. We must resist the urge to simply dream at a level that won't disappoint others or bring unwanted criticism. So, you will have to keep going back and forth to the fields, make the drive every day to the office, show up to the classroom, or keep the home in order while being the only one who still sees the possibilities. This is not about trying to change the responses of others or even persuade the crowds that are the closest. It's not always about helping others see what they can't. Remember this was a dream not for his father, not for his brother, but it was given to Joseph. It is about how we respond to God's dream for our lives. Even when no one else can see it, will we believe it? Do you believe it? Do you still believe that God has a bigger picture for your life? Do you believe it, even if you can't fully see it at this moment?

CHAPTER 2

I'M A
SURVIVOR

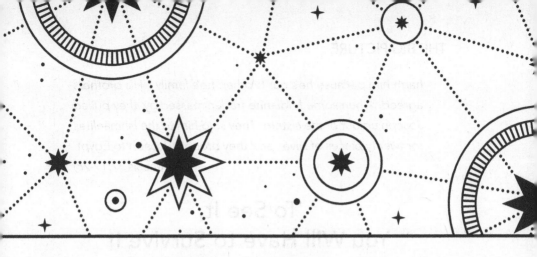

CHAPTER 2
I'M A SURVIVOR
Jevon

The brothers said to each other, "Here comes the big dreamer. Come on now, let's kill him and throw him into one of the cisterns, and we'll say a wild animal devoured him. Then we will see what becomes of his dreams!"

When Reuben heard what they said, he saved him from them, telling them, "Let's not take his life." Reuben said to them, "Don't spill his blood! Throw him into this desert cistern, but don't lay a hand on him." He intended to save Joseph from them and take him back to his father.

When Joseph reached his brothers, they stripped off Joseph's long robe, took him, and threw him into the cistern, an empty cistern with no water in it. When they sat down to eat, they looked up and saw a caravan of Ishmaelites coming from Gilead, with camels carrying sweet resin, medicinal resin, and fragrant resin on their way down to Egypt. Judah said to his brothers, "What do we gain if we kill our brother and hide his blood? Come on, let's sell him to the Ishmaelites. Let's not harm him because he's our brother; he's family." His brothers agreed. When some Midianite traders passed by, they pulled Joseph up out of the cistern. They sold him to the Ishmaelites for twenty pieces of silver, and they brought Joseph to Egypt.

(Genesis 37:19-28)

To See It, You Will Have to Survive It

Destiny's Child released their hot single "Survivor" in 2001. It's hard to believe that was over twenty years ago. However, I do recall that this song became an anthem for women across the world. Beyoncé, a member of the group at the time, was gaining worldwide appeal, and the song resonated with people from around the globe. It seemed to strike a familiar chord with its listeners. The song placed a spotlight on the strength of a woman after a messy breakup. It took one through the emotional strain of separation, while proclaiming and celebrating one's sense of determination that holds us together during such times. The lyrics affirmed that the woman was better, stronger, richer, wiser, smarter. It sold nine million records. There was much to love about the song, but it was the chorus that was the most memorable:

> I'm a survivor, I'm gonna make it
> I will survive, keep on survivin'[3]

You don't have to be a fan of Beyoncé or Destiny's Child to embrace the importance of the song's message. Every dreamer needs to hear this chorus at least once. Many of those dots that appear in our lives can be difficult. They will represent obstacles to overcome. They are the moments that are going to be painful. They are agonizing and uncomfortable. However, they play a necessary role in the larger picture. Finding God's dream for your life will require you to survive something. There is no escaping or delaying this reality. To see it, you will have to survive it.

It's tempting to start drawing the dream without connecting the obstacles. These are the dots we want to delete from the picture. They are the moments that we often pray would cease. We meticulously try to forge our image with as few of these moments as possible. And yet, without them, the picture is incomplete. Surviving is a part of every dreamer's experience. We pride ourselves on being dreamers. We celebrate the dreamers in our community. Undoubtedly, behind every dreamer is a survivor.

This was certainly true for Joseph. He had been equipped with a dream that no one could understand. The ones who hated him couldn't see it. His father, who loved him, couldn't see it either. In fact, dreaming didn't make Joseph's life easier; it only made it more difficult. It caused more tension within his family. It brought more questions than answers. The dreams shed light on the unhealthy dynamics already present in his life and environment. They made him rethink and reimagine his life forever. Things would get worse before they got better.

His brothers saw Joseph from a distance, and the mocking commenced. "Here comes that dreamer," they professed. "Here comes Joseph with his fancy coat, warm coffee, and clipboard ready to spy on us again." Their dislike for him had escalated. This was more than just the typical family drama and sibling rivalry. It evolved to the point where they began devising a plan to take Joseph's life. This seems extreme. The response does not fit the crime. He dreamed big, and they planned to kill him. They had several other options at their disposal. They could have all agreed to give him the silent treatment.

They could have mocked him, scared him, or taught him a lesson by showing him that there were ten of them and only one of him. I could understand if they wanted to scare him or teach him a lesson he would never forget. These were at least reasonable, considering the jealously they were experiencing.

Their anger and jealousy, escalating to hatred, is unfortunate, to put it mildly, but Joseph was not necessarily the cause of their anger or their feelings of frustration. One could make the argument that Joseph was simply a casualty of proximity. This argument is a prime example of misdirected anger. It's what occurs when our feelings go unchecked and unresolved, and finally boil over into extreme action.

For years the brothers watched their father display a different kind of love and affection toward Joseph. Remember, Joseph was the younger brother who received his father's attention. It was a love that stood out. While a father's love toward a child sounds endearing, it was infuriating to Joseph's siblings. Why couldn't they receive that kind of treatment? Why was Joseph so deserving of this outward display of affection? The mere presence of Joseph was a constant reminder of what they could not obtain. The special coat that Jacob gave Joseph was a sign of it too. They could not direct their anger at their father, so they chose Joseph as the more likely target. Unchecked feelings can quickly lead to impulsive decisions.

The problem with anger is not always the intensity of the emotion, but the direction in which it is focused. Unfortunately, the people closest to us are often the ones we tend to hurt the most. The people who bear the brunt of our anger are usually the people in close proximity.

Anger always needs a target, and one way or another it will find a way to get expressed. When we can't or won't address the reason for the frustration, we just search for the closest target. If we can't express it on our job, the people in our homes become the target. If we can't bring it home, we carry it to houses of worship. If we can't carry it to church, we bring to the line at the grocery store. If we can't take it there, we just turn it inward. This reality challenges us to be aware and courageous enough to deal with our issues, to recognize and address the true source of our anger, so that our kids, spouses, friends, and even coworkers don't have to feel as if they are merely target practice.

When we don't effectively deal with these unresolved issues, somebody in our present can say a word that triggers something from our past, and then we search for a target. It's why a colorful coat can be the source of hate and division in God's chosen family. It's why a simple dream can raise the level of hate. That's how a group of brothers can see their younger sibling off in the distance and start to orchestrate a plot to take his life.

Pits and Dark Places

When Joseph arrives and greets his brothers, they strip him of his coat and throw him into a pit. They leave him there to die. This person in the pit is a far cry from the one we just met who talked about God's dream for his life. It's not adding up. The dots aren't connecting.

This was not part of the picture, so he thought. When God gave Joseph a glimpse of things to come, God showed him an exciting future and a hopeful image. Joseph was in a position of power. He mattered. He was important. There was no mention of him fighting for his life at the bottom of a pit. No one glues this image onto their vision boards. Pits are not part of New Year's resolutions. It's not included in the goals we share with loved ones. There were several possible, natural, next steps to seeing this bigger picture God had for his life. Being at the bottom of a pit was not one of them. It's not a dot most would expect. It's proof that if Joseph knew every detail, he might abandon this journey.

It's not what we want or expect when we connect the dots, but no one is exempt from finding oneself in a dark place and hitting rock bottom. Money cannot shield us. Fame does not exempt us. Faith does not make us immune. There are some pits that we find ourselves in because of our decision-making. We make bad choices and suffer the consequences. Then there are other pits outside of our control. There are ones we are born into and others we are hired into. Some pits are the private struggles we battle behind closed doors. We've learned how to mask the darkness with smiles, makeup, and crisp haircuts. We attend to our daily rituals and perform our routines as if they don't exist. And yet, we are one argument, one comment, and one letdown away from falling apart. It's an Oscar-worthy performance.

We also can't forget about those pits we are called to live out in public. These are the pits that we want to hide, but we must live them out before public opinion. These pits are the times when we fail or experience hardship, and everybody knows about it. It's when our lowest point becomes the topic of conversation and interesting content at the dinner table for others.

Then there are pits that are more systematic. These are policies, practices, and procedures that continue to affect people's lives for decades. They transcend individual feelings and personal decisions but rise to the very fabric of how our lives are lived.

Exit Doors

A significant characteristic of a pit is that there is no way out. The pit represents those moments in our lives that we can't escape. We want to leave, but there are no exit doors. We cannot navigate our way through a difficult experience, and we feel stuck.

The specific dimensions of Joseph's pit are unclear. We aren't told how wide or deep it was. Some suggest it could have been an old well. One thing that is certain is that he's stuck. It's deep enough that he can't climb out on his own. He wants to escape, but he can't. He wants to be liberated, but no path leads up or out. It's frustrating when you want to leave but can't.

This is not an experience to which we are accustomed. Pay attention the next time you enter a public space. There will be multiple indicators highlighting the closest exit doors. The bright-red or neon orange exit signs will be hard to miss. For fear of a fire or any other emergency, someone has already pre-planned your exit. They have thought through every detail. The route has been predetermined. The doors have been prefabricated for accessibility. These planners even added an emergency light in case the room or building is darkened, or there is a power outage. In today's culture, codes and laws are in place to ensure proper exits in case of an emergency.

Sometimes there's just no escape.

If only this applied to every room or situation where we've landed. It certainly doesn't apply to pits. Sometimes there's just no escape from the painful circumstances that we experience.

It's where many people find themselves even today—wanting to leave but unable to locate the exit doors. The desire to escape is present, but the possibilities of leaving or things improving are not visible.

It's difficult for anyone to be stuck. We immediately start looking for the dots that could serve as an exit strategy. We summon our inner MacGyvers and start plotting the course. We will do or say just about anything. Who can we call? What can we try? We look for the smallest opening to yield a proper exit.

Pits are doable when we can connect the dots that lead out of them. We can bear what seems to be temporary. We can count down the days and find something to entertain our anxieties. But what happens when the dots don't connect? How will we respond when the exit signs are not lit, and exit strategies fail?

This can be a trying time for anyone. It's frustrating. It happens in relationships. It occurs in professions. It exists in just about every area of our lives. We arrive at a place where we hopelessly proclaim, "This is the way it will always be." It must have seemed that way for Joseph, and often seems that way for us. There was no logical exit door that he could see or even imagine.

Nourished

The text reminds us that there was "no water in [the cistern]" (Genesis 37:24). It's a small but important detail. On the one hand, it meant that Joseph would not drown—a possibility if the pit was indeed a well. But on the other hand, it meant there was nothing inside this pit that had the ability to nourish him. It's another aspect of our pit that makes them untenable. Eventually, he would die of thirst and starvation. The human body can sustain itself without many things, but it can't function long without water and food. This pit could not sustain Joseph.

While food and water are absolutely necessary to living, there are other aspects to our personalities and spiritual journeys that are just as essential. In Philippians 4:19, Paul promises that "My God will meet your every need out of his riches in the glory that is found in Christ Jesus." This not only hints at God's willingness and ability to provide, but it speaks to our variety of needs. Our needs extend far beyond the basics of food and water. Our souls and spirits need more. Your faith needs more. Relationally you need more. Some of us need to be in places that serve a higher purpose beyond ourselves. Some need to feel like their voices matter. Others need a challenge. Some individuals need clear signs of verbal affirmation. There are some seasons where we need rest and to be refueled. Look back at your dots and reflect on the things in your past that have sustained and nourished you. What have you needed along your spiritual journey? What do you presently need? What seems trivial to some could be essential to others. If we are not honest about these needs, it's easy to find ourselves at the bottom of pits and starving spiritually or emotionally.

Pits affirm this notion. They starve us of the very things that sustain us. Are you currently in a place where you feel starved? Is the hard place sustaining or life-giving? Or does it feel like you are malnourished, and if it goes on too long, you won't make it?

The pits are where we feel disconnected from the very things that give us energy and life. Most know how to ask and articulate when there is a lack of food or water, yet we often become apprehensive about expressing and advocating for the other necessities that we desperately need. Acknowledging the need helps us articulate this to others and to ourselves. It helps us to identify pits where the pay is impressive. We can identify those dark places even in positions of power and importance. It gives one the language to articulate when our relationships have run dry and need to be rekindled. It speaks to the seasons and places of our lives that no longer sustain us. Our souls get tired, and they long for cisterns full of water.

Intervention

If you've never seen the show *Intervention*, each episode has a similar theme. There usually is one individual suffering from some form of addiction or substance abuse, which has become detrimental to their well-being and the health of the people around them. At some point, their loved ones make a collective decision to intervene because the situation has reached a point where the individual needs outside assistance. They can't do it by themselves; they need others to hold them accountable. They need someone else to remind them who they used to be, and someone or something from the outside to help get them to a better place.

As this breaking point is reached, the person's support system reaches out for help and strategizes how to get their loved one into the same room with all of them together. It's here that they share their concerns, their love for the person, and their fear if the behavior continues. This is when the family and friends reveal to the person that this is an intervention. Even if you haven't seen the show, it's not an unfamiliar theme. The intervention is necessary because the individual is no longer capable of doing what's needed alone. The person needs outside help.

Joseph needs an intervention. He needs someone or something from the outside to assist him in getting out of this pit. The situation is beyond his abilities. He doesn't know enough to think his way out. He is not physically strong enough to pull himself up from this dark place. There are no exit doors, and he will likely starve or die of thirst. Joseph is alone, and there is absolutely nothing he can do to change his condition. He can't raise himself from the pit, though it's not from a lack of effort or an unwillingness to escape. It's just a difficult reminder that some pits are beyond our control. They exhaust our mental abilities. They are beyond the capacities of our resources and connection. We can't think our way out. We can't pay our way out. It will require something that is beyond what we have to give.

It's why one of the most helpful prayers that we can ever recite is this: "God, I can't do it by myself, and I need your help." (Please read and recite that again.) It's an admission of total surrender. This prayer is not a comfortable one. It's accepting the realization that we have exhausted all of our options and need help. It's a confession that we don't readily admit. It seems weak. It sounds like we are waving a white flag. We pride ourselves on being self-sufficient, independent, and self-reliant. While those traits are admirable, there are a lot of people with all of these characteristics who are still stuck in a dark place. Our need to display our strength turns into an unhealthy form of stubbornness. We convince ourselves that special rewards are given to those who aren't reliant on anybody or anything.

Joseph reveals a different truth. The essence of strength is not always centered around the gift of self. Strength is also surrendering. It's being willing to lose control and trust in something outside of ourselves. True strength is displayed in the willingness to accept the help that invites God to intervene in our lives. God wants to come into our lives. God doesn't just want to intervene through the dreams. God wants to intervene in the dark places where few want to visit. Are there areas of your life where you need God to intervene? Are there situations that are beyond your control, and you need help? It's OK to admit. It's acceptable and even encouraged to ask.

Strength is also surrendering. It's being willing to lose control and trust in something outside of ourselves.

God wants to intervene in those places where we are ashamed for others to see. The prayer "God, I need your help" is not a declaration of giving up, but an invitation. It's acknowledging that this pit is beyond our abilities and inviting the presence of God into that space. The only thing we can control is our willingness to survive.

He Survived

Our first response to the pit is to try to understand it. We want to make sense out of it and find purpose in this pit. It's the cause of questions similar to "Why me?" "Why now?" "What is God trying to teach me?" While these are valid questions, they are not always helpful.

As the reader, we don't get any insight into what Joseph was thinking down in the pit, how he interprets it, or how it affects him mentally and emotionally. We get this from so many other biblical characters, but not Joseph. We are left wondering. What did Joseph think about his current situation?

Maybe his lack of commentary could be an answer in itself. Perhaps Joseph is not at a place where he's seeking to understand the pit, because he is just trying to survive. It's tempting to become reflective in similar situations. The assumption is that our understanding will yield a sense of endurance and strength waiting to be unleashed. We try to connect the dots to and from our pits.

At the moment, Joseph has no idea how and where this will end. He can't understand it. However, he can survive it. Joseph gives us a needed reminder that you can survive those moments when you do not understand. Comprehension is not a prerequisite for survival.

You can survive those moments when you do not understand.

Figure it out at another time, just don't give up. The answers may arrive years later. It will make sense one day, but maybe not today. Place your energies on getting out and getting help. Joseph's only task in the pit was survival. Scriptures give a healthy reminder, "Therefore, stop worrying about tomorrow, because tomorrow will worry about itself. Each day has enough trouble of its own" (Matthew 6:34). It's so tempting to keep looking ahead, but that alone can send us deeper into the pit.

37

Looking ahead can be overwhelming. Joseph only had to endure for another day, one day at a time. We don't know how long he was in the pit, though it seems like a short time in the text. It probably felt like a lifetime to Joseph. But as he learned, all it takes is one day for our lives to take a turn for the worse. Conversely, all it takes is one day, one moment, to make a shift for something different. Just one day. In one day, you can get a call back that you didn't expect. In one day, you can receive news that will dramatically change your life. It's an invitation to hold on to something that inspires us. Maybe it's something exciting. It could be something hopeful. It could be a reminder of a bigger picture.

One minute Joseph is in the pit alone, and the next moment, off in the distance, he starts hearing familiar voices. Was he hallucinating? Was it a false alarm? Were his brothers back to finish the job? He doesn't know if these voices are hopeful or fearful. He doesn't know whether to be excited or anxious. Apparently, someone had been working on Joseph's exit strategy. His brothers return to the pit and find that Joseph is still alive. He survived. They peered into a dark place and still saw signs of life.

Joseph was thrown into a pit, left to die, but in the end, he was still able to be rescued. Rescue is a central theme that is carried out through the entire biblical text. It's a needed reminder that we are never too far gone to be rescued or to be offered redemption when we have hit rock bottom. The realization that redemptive power is available gives us the courage to look for life in difficult places, and the courage to ask for help to climb out of dark situations.

Considering the circumstances, Joseph was lucky to be alive. The odds were stacked against him. The survival rate was not in his favor. He survived being trapped in a pit. He survived a murder plot against him. It was ten brothers against one. He had no food. No water. No friends. He survived the jealous and impulsive decisions of his older brothers. He survived their misguided anger. He survived when there was no clear exit. He could have easily died in that pit. However, he made it. Survival, by itself, was a success.

Joseph's survival invites us to reflect and remember our own places of survival. Joseph was a survivor, and so is each one of us. You made it. You survived it. Take a moment to consider the obstacles that you've had to endure. Think about the challenges, the disappointments, and the letdowns.

This past year has been one of survival for many people. Numerous individuals have suffered the loss of jobs, loss of loved ones, loss of homes, and loss of everything familiar. Every single day, people are dealing with addictions, health concerns, and family drama. Any one or a combination of these situations could have easily crushed someone's spirit, hopes, and even their future. It could have, but it didn't. That alone has to be enough. Survival is a success. These are the dots that can't be overlooked because they serve as reminders not of what happened to us, but of how God has rescued us.

I remember watching the 1992 Olympics and witnessing an unforgettable story. Derek Redmond of Great Britain was running the 400-meter race in Barcelona. Keep in mind that these athletes train for years, but each individual race takes seconds to finish. For many athletes, participating in the Olympics is a dream come true. However, in the middle of this particular race, Redmond was injured. He immediately started grabbing the back of his leg, and the remaining runners finished the race as he collapsed onto the track. He found enough strength to stand to his feet and started limping his way down the track. The crowd rose to their feet and cheered him on. His father ran onto the track to help his son finish the race. He finally made it across the finish line with tears in his eyes, being held by his father. It was the worst time he had ever run. Would anyone call him a quitter? I think not. Why? Simply because he made it. He finished. He survived.

Merely surviving is counterintuitive from what we've been taught. Our culture is obsessed with thriving. There are no book shortages on how to succeed and be successful. It's what everyone wants to know. We want to be fruitful in every aspect of our lives. We want to thrive in our marriages. We want to flourish as parents. We want to succeed at our jobs. We want our faith to grow to the kind that moves mountains. The next time you visit your local bookstore, take a glance at the business or leadership section and look for this theme.

In the later chapters, we will highlight other dots in Joseph's life where he thrives in very difficult situations. There is nothing wrong with thriving or with being successful. It speaks to God's ability to bless us in all circumstances. Joseph's life will give witness to this. But for now, success is defined by his willingness to survive. It's seen in his ability to make it out alive. Let that be enough. Sometimes, survival alone is success. It's not the book that we write afterward. It's not the lecture we give about it or the social media campaign that brought attention to our condition. It's not the monetary gain that followed that defines a successful survival. For Joseph, success was simply making it out alive. Being in a dark place with no exit door, with nothing to sustain him, and desperately in need of an intervention, he was still alive when his brothers pulled him out of the pit. And that alone is enough. He survived it. Joseph survived being in a difficult place. He survived the darkness. He survived every plan designed to destroy him and to kill his dream. He still had his life, and they could not touch his dream. I'd say that's a win. When you think it's not enough, reflect on the number of persons who have gone through similar experiences and did not have a similar outcome.

Remember also that Joseph did not survive one pit, but two. The other pit is the one he was born into, with a dysfunctional family dynamic and limited possibilities for his future. God doesn't just save us from things. God saves us from people. Not imaginary people or abstract relationships. These are people with first and last names. They have actual birthdates and unique personalities. In fact, real people create real environments. Joseph's life with his father and brothers would never be a place conducive to God's dream for his life.

The danger that he faces is being saved from one pit only to be trapped in a different one that is even more dangerous. His brothers pulled him out of one pit but he could not avoid returning to the same dysfunctional and toxic environment. The pit in the ground lasted a few days; the pit of his family would last a lifetime.

This pit would include daily starvation of the very things that would give him life. He would be cut off from being the person whom God created him to be. He would forever be a dreamer who couldn't dream. It's unfortunate, but the only place he couldn't dream was in his own home. This is not a situation that showed any signs of improvement. He's stuck in a place where there is no way out; there are no exit doors. He's never going to be nourished by this community. Joseph's only hope was a divine intervention.

These are the pits that are often too hard to name and recognize. They are not hidden away or in deserted wastelands. In these pits, the lights are always on, and the furniture is meticulously placed. The street names are familiar, and the neighbors smile and wave. Underneath the familiar is a realization that staying would mean starving. One could be in this pit for decades and never realize it. It takes some individuals years to admit that everything can't grow everywhere.

Last summer, we hired a landscaper to do some work in our backyard. I was impressed by his calculations and attention to detail. He noted where the sun rose, where it set, and the amount of direct sunlight given to this area. We had our suggestions for what we wanted to be planted. (I use "we" very liberally here.) We did research online. We knew the colors we wanted. We got ideas by scouting the yards of others. We gave him a list of what we wanted to plant...which he politely rejected. He affirmed our taste but acknowledged that the environment wasn't conducive to our selections.

Similarly, this is what life in that other pit, the one Joseph was born into, was like. If he returned to his old life with his family, for the rest of his life Joseph would have to suppress the best parts of himself in order to fit in and make those around him comfortable. If Joseph was ever going to see this dream fulfilled, it would not be here. Surviving this pit he was thrown into was a necessary dot, even if it was a painful one.

We All Have a Role to Play

While it's easy to cast judgment on Joseph's brothers, there are more similarities between them and us than we often admit. It's easy to place ourselves in the role of Joseph. We naturally cast ourselves in the position of the dreamer who has been wronged. And we should. We can relate to much of his story. Being in a pit is a familiar experience that many have had to endure. However, everyone can't play the role of Joseph in every scenario. We can't always be the people who are cast into the pit. Someone had to make the suggestion to attack Joseph. Another had to rob him of his coat. Someone had to push him into that dark place. Someone had to remain silent.

Even the best of us oscillates between living as Joseph and operating as his brothers. There are moments when we have been shoved into unwanted places. At other times, we were guilty of pushing others inside. At some point in our lives, we have thrown someone into a ditch. We were the dream killers because of something we said or didn't say, the result of our actions, or because we failed to act. Whether it was intentional or not, it still hurt. There have been others who thought they couldn't grow in our vicinity. We created unhealthy environments for the visions of others. They needed refuge from our insecurities. Their dreams and inspiration starved in our presence. They couldn't evolve. They could not fully be who and what God created them to be. The tables turned. They prayed that God would rescue them from us. Someone has prayed that prayer about us. They sought freedom from us. Deliverance for them meant distance from us. We were the brothers and didn't know it.

Perhaps we were not the ones who directly led to Joseph's demise, but how often have we stood idle while others were knowingly being injured. Verse 25 describes a chilling scene. While they have committed to letting their brother die in a pit, Joseph's brothers are seen sitting down and eating dinner. It's as if nothing has changed! They have returned to their everyday lives and aren't bothered by the reality that nearby someone is dying in a dark place. It's troubling to think they could so easily compartmentalize what was happening. Did they just go back out into the fields every day while he was down there? Did they carry on the same conversations? They didn't even lose their appetite! How could they?

It's a fair question that we must turn inward. While we may not be so direct in the environments that we create, our silence speaks volumes. It moves beyond the individual and has communal implications. It's so easy to go about our lives and forget about the pain of those near us. We forget about the students and teachers in our community who don't have access to proper resources. We forget about the communities that fear being targeted because of their accents or the color of their skin. We forget about the abuse that has been done to people because of their gender or sexual preference. We sit down at our dinner tables with a clear conscience. We approach our beautiful sanctuaries to sing our inspirational songs free from the anxieties of the world around us. It's easy to become calloused to the pain that surrounds us. It's even tempting to think that Joseph deserved to be there. If only he had kept his dreams to himself. If only he was not so arrogant. Can't you hear the excuses? No one asks to be in a pit. No one wants to be the object of discrimination or hate. No one desires to be marginalized or begs to die.

However, all it took was one person to care. Just one. One person turned the tide. Judah reminded his brothers of their humanity and their relationship to the one in the pit. Judah wasn't perfect. His mind was on profit, just as much as it was on saving his brother's life. But he did care; he did have a shred of compassion, and that was enough to make a difference for Joseph.

Pulling him out of that pit was a saving moment for Joseph, but it was also a saving moment for the brothers as well. It was God's way of rescuing them from the worst of their sins and decisions. Joseph's brothers have done nothing deserving of a second chance. They tried to kill Joseph. They mocked him. They attempted to cover up their actions. But by sparing Joseph's life, they spare themselves from the sin of murder. They aren't yet aware of this redeeming moment in their lives. Remember life is lived forward but understood backward. This should be encouraging for us. Our sins and mistakes could and should have discounted us from many blessings and opportunities. However, we are still here. We made it by God's grace, and God continues to give us another chance. We are here today because we too have survived our sins and decisions. By God's grace, we are survivors.

We are here today because we too have survived our sins and decisions. By God's grace, we are survivors.

Fill in the Blank

My mother is a cancer survivor, and I've always been amazed at how easily this becomes part of one's identity. The phrase "cancer survivor" becomes a lifelong affirmation of what the individual has overcome. The process of acknowledging it is admirable. Depending on the method of treatment, the patient gets an opportunity to ring a bell at its conclusion. For many people, this is a big deal. It's the moment of celebration that the individual gets to experience as they complete a portion of their treatment. It's believed that this tradition of ringing bells started a few decades ago, when an admiral in the US Navy was undergoing radiation therapy for his own cancer treatment. He informed his doctor that he wanted to follow the Navy tradition of the bells to signify "when the job was done." When his treatment was nearing its end, he brought a brass bell, rang it several times, and left it as a donation. They mounted his bell on the wall, and the tradition became contagious. It spread to different hospitals in the area and eventually became a common practice. Ringing the bell celebrates surviving.

In light of that tradition, let this be a reminder that you are a survivor. Take the prerogative to personalize the phrase. Maybe you are a grief survivor, abuse survivor, church hurt survivor, divorce survivor, or low self-esteem survivor. The options are many; just fill in the blank. Regardless of how you describe it, let this be a part of your identity. Not because you are defined by it, but because it's a constant reminder of what you have been able to overcome with God's help. After surviving the pit, Joseph knows and can remind himself that there isn't anything he can't overcome. When there was no way out, nothing to nourish him, God intervened and pulled him out. You have survived situations that you never imagined you would have to endure. To all the survivors, find a bell and ring it as loud as you can. Celebrate that you made it.

CHAPTER 3
DREAMING IN PRISON

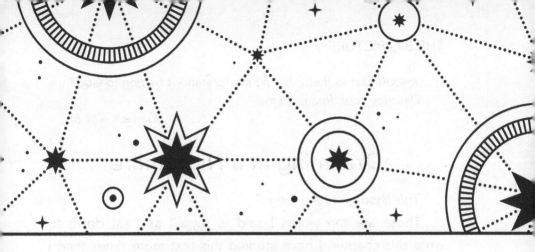

CHAPTER 3
DREAMING
IN PRISON
Nicole

Some time later, both the wine steward and the baker for Egypt's king offended their master, the king of Egypt. Pharaoh was angry with his two officers, the chief wine steward and the chief baker, and he put them under arrest with the commander of the royal guard in the same jail where Joseph was imprisoned. The commander of the royal guard assigned Joseph to assist them. After they had been under arrest for some time, both of them—the wine steward and the baker for Egypt's king who were imprisoned in the jail—had dreams one night, and each man's dream had its own meaning. When Joseph met them in the morning, he saw that they were upset. He asked the officers of Pharaoh who were under arrest with him in his master's house, "Why do you look so distressed today?"

They answered, "We've both had dreams, but there's no one to interpret them."

Joseph said to them, "Don't interpretations belong to God?
Describe your dreams to me."

(Genesis 40:1-8)

Dreaming in a Nightmare

This shouldn't take long.

Those are the words I said to myself as I sat down to write this chapter. I have studied this text more times than I can count, and it has all the hallmark characteristics of what any preaching professor would call "fertile ground." Is this an impossible situation where only divine intervention could change things? Yes! Is this a flawed but faithful protagonist who sincerely desires God's will in their lives? Absolutely! Is this a long-standing dream or promise that has yet to be realized? That's three for three!

I thought I'd place my fingertips on the keyboard and take divine dictation as the Holy Spirit sent paragraphs straight from heaven's library. Yet, something else happened—or to be more precise, something didn't happen. Try as I might, hour after hour, the blank page stared back at me, and not a single sentence would come. At first, I thought it was just your typical writer's block, but when the same thing happened the next day, and the next day, and the week after that, I knew that something else was wrong. The truth is, *I was struggling to write about dreams because I've been a witness to so many nightmares.*

As a pastor, I'm called to sit with people in the darkest places of their lives. These are places where dreams shatter, hope is buried alive, and promise seems forever lost. In these places, you pray with parents whose small child had a heart attack. You break the news to a sick mother that her only daughter has been killed. You counsel a couple who are contemplating divorce, pray for a teenager who has entered rehab for the second time, or search for safe housing for an abused mother and her four children. This boulevard of broken dreams has only been made longer by a global pandemic that has taken lives, stolen precious time, and upended our way of being, living, worshiping—and, I dare say, dreaming. How can you dream when life itself is so uncertain? How can you dream when what you trusted in is no longer trustworthy? How can you dream when you're living in a nightmare? I'm not sure how to answer those questions, but Joseph is.

Conditions and Character

When we first met Joseph, he was a coffee-toting, colored-coat-wearing, tattle-telling dreamer. In my scriptural imagination, Joseph has shoulder-length golden-brown hair that he tosses to one side just as he gets to the part of the dream where all of his brothers are bowing down to him. I have no scriptural evidence to support this, but in my mind, that's Joseph. Then we move to another dot. The dot where he was pulled out of the pit that his jealous brothers threw him into. The dot where he survived what tried to kill him and was sold into slavery in Egypt. It's in this dot where it seems like the other ones are starting to line up. God's dream for Joseph's life is beginning to take shape. It didn't begin as Joseph would have guessed, but now he's starting to see some of it. Joseph is sold as a slave in the household of an Egyptian official named Potiphar.

The dots keep connecting, and Joseph rises through the ranks until he's managing Potiphar's entire household. Scripture says that Potiphar didn't even know what was happening in his home, he had such complete trust and confidence in his servant Joseph. And I'm sure that when Joseph lay down at night, he couldn't help feeling like his dreams were on schedule. He dreamed he'd be a leader; he dreamed he'd be ruling over others and look at him now! Joseph is leading the household of an officer in the court of the most powerful country in the ancient Near East!

Dreams do come true. Dots do line up…until they don't. Without warning, the dots began to disconnect, and what looked like a dream became a nightmare. Potiphar's wife relentlessly pursued Joseph, and when he wouldn't agree to an affair, she framed him for assault. And now, Joseph finds himself in a dungeon jail, likely beneath the officer's home where he used to be in charge. Perhaps, Joseph is hearing the padded footsteps of the people he used to lead, moving to and fro overhead.

Joseph's experience may seem extreme because, one hopes, none of us lives in an episode of *The Young and the Restless* or has been thrown into dungeons, yet that doesn't mean that life hasn't disconnected the dots for us in other, less dramatic ways. While God gives us dreams, God doesn't guarantee that living them will be easy. Each of us has had those seasons where it seems like all the dots are lining up, where things are finally falling into place, and that's when we get the call about the accident. That's when we leave the doctor's office with the diagnosis. That's when the marriage is heading toward divorce. That's when the company begins downsizing. That's when the variant starts to spread. That's when the dream becomes a nightmare.

If we're not careful, we can forget how to dream at times like these. We can descend into dungeons too dark for us to see the dots connecting. We can forget that there was once a time when we imagined the impossible and expected God to make it happen.

That's where some of us stay. That's where some of us are right now. But not Joseph. Joseph teaches us through this text how to keep dreaming in a nightmare. The first lesson is this: don't let your conditions determine your character. Joseph is in prison. You might expect him to assimilate to the reality of his condition. After all, he's around people who may have committed heinous crimes, and this sheltered, teenage boy may not have the street smarts to navigate a dungeon jail. Maybe he ought to change the way he walks or talks to demonstrate his strength, so that other prisoners won't think he's someone to be taken advantage of. It's survival of the fittest in the prisons of life's circumstances, and to make it, you may have to make yourself over too.

Don't let your conditions determine your character.

But not Joseph. At the end of chapter 39, we have a déjà vu moment where we learn that Joseph has been appointed as a leader, even in prison. Just as he dreamed of being a leader of his brothers, just as he became the leader of Potiphar's house, he's appointed as a leader in the prison. Wherever he goes, he's like cream in the coffee rising to the top. We often talk about the dreams of Joseph, but we fail to remember the character of Joseph. When the dots seem disconnected, the temptation is to let our circumstances determine who we are. We may let our condition determine our character. But Joseph is a leader no matter what, no matter where, and no matter who's watching. And perhaps the question for us today is not whether or not we are holding on to our dream, but rather, are we holding on to our character?

If God said you are a leader, then are you leading only when you have the power?

If God said you are a builder, are you building only when you have the position?

If God said you are a dreamer, are you dreaming only when things are perfect?

Or are you whom God says you are, no matter where you are?

The key to holding on to our dreams does not depend on whether or not all the dots are connected, but whether our character is consistent. That's easy to write, but it's much harder to live. When life takes you to the dungeon depths of pain, loss, grief, anger, or fear, it's easy to forget who you are.

Montez did. I first met Montez at a storytelling showcase highlighting experiences of incarceration. He shared that when he was a child, we all would have "rolled our eyes at him." As a star athlete, class president, and self-described teacher's pet, there was nothing he didn't do well. His teachers constantly affirmed him as a leader, and even nicknamed him "Mr. President."

Things changed right before high school. Montez's grandmother suddenly died, and he moved to a new neighborhood with an uncle and his brothers. In this neighborhood, gang activity was rampant, and the teacher's pet was soon dealing drugs and committing petty robberies. At sixteen, he participated in a robbery where one of his fellow gang members shot and killed someone. As an accessory to the crime, he was arrested, tried, convicted, and sent to prison for fifteen to twenty-five years. The change of Montez's conditions caused him to lose sight of his character.

Some of his former gang members advised him to immediately find members of his old crew to connect with in prison. He might need to beat someone up, get a tattoo, or some other test of loyalty to survive prison. But before he could find someone who looked familiar, he learned that he looked familiar to someone else. A deep, booming voice shouted across the yard, "Well, if it isn't Mr. President!" The voice revealed a vaguely familiar face of someone who said he remembered Montez from their elementary school days. Before Montez could utter a response, the man pulled a stack of letters from his back pocket and said, "You still know everything, Mr. President? Well, tell me exactly what this says." Montez read him the letters, and later helped him write a response. Word spread, and other inmates began to seek appointments with "Mr. President" to help them with various things.

Relating the story with tears streaming down his face, Montez shared that it was behind bars, among a group of men whose dreams seemed irretrievably broken, that he recovered his own dream. He may have been a prisoner, but to some he was Mr. President. He was someone who had knowledge, someone who could lead, someone who could help others and speak for them. He remembered the character God had given him, and in doing so began to recover the dream God had given him too. He enrolled in college courses, founded a literacy program for his fellow inmates, and helped organize a board that represented concerns to the prison leadership. When he was released, he was hired as a gang interventionist and given the title "President of New Purposes." He howled with laughter and said, "You see...Even in prison, you'll still find a president."

I wonder what prison you may find yourself in today. I wonder what challenge, setback, or even mistake finds you locked out of your preferred present. Whatever it is, you can still hold on to your dream in prison if you hold to who you are. Your conditions don't define you. You define them. If you can hold on to your character, you can hold on to your dream.

Looking Beneath the Surface

Joseph's life teaches us that one way to hold on to our dreams in prison is to maintain our character. There's just one little, teeny-tiny problem: it's hard to maintain our character when on the surface, our dreams look dead. We may not notice the timeline in our text at first glance. Yet, biblical scholars contend that the time between the end of chapter 39 and the beginning of chapter 40 could be as many as ten years!

That's 120 months, 520 weeks, 3,650 days, 5,256,000 minutes. Ten years is a long time to wait, a long time to be stuck. And despite maintaining his character, it doesn't seem like the dots have started connecting. No, he's still in the same place and the same dark dungeon where dreams die.

Yet, it's in this place that we learn: we can hold on to our dreams in prison if we don't mistake dormancy for death.

Recently, I hired a landscaping company for what can only be described as an intervention. I should be in a dungeon myself because I'm guilty of multiple herbal homicides. I have murdered many plants in the first degree. It's hard to admit, but I've got quite a rap sheet. I've killed plants in pots. I've slaughtered entire garden beds. I even managed to plant a tree that the nursery owner said was *impossible* to kill, and it too died. But there's one plant that has survived even my murderous green thumb.

In our first home in New Jersey, there were hostas. Some people love hostas. They are a reliable and sturdy annual that requires little care. Yet, for me, they took up too much space, and I wanted more colorful and bold flowers. One spring, I took a shovel, dug up the hostas, and planted rows and rows of my beautiful, colorful flowers in their place. A few weeks later, when I came to the crime scene of my garden, every flower I planted had gone on to be with the Lord, except one: I was in shock to find big, beautiful, blooming hostas!

I couldn't understand it! How could this plant still be alive? I had dug it up myself! I couldn't figure it out, so I called my neighbor, a far more experienced gardener than I was, to explain this plant resurrection phenomenon. He said I had made a novice gardener mistake: I had removed only what looked dead on the surface.

What I couldn't see underneath were the roots that laid dormant but not dead. The roots were preserving the nutrients, energy, and substance to sustain the life of this plant—even though I'd done my best to kill it—and waited until the season changed and new shoots of hosta leaves emerged. What I thought was dead was living underneath the surface.

Perhaps, that's the message God wants to remind you of today. I know it's been months; I know it's been years, and it doesn't seem like anything is happening on the surface. But, if you remember nothing else, remember this:

Your dreams are not done; they're just dormant.

Your dreams are not denied; they're just dormant.

Your dreams are not dead; they're just dormant.

Your dreams are not dead; they're just dormant.

Underneath the surface, where you and I cannot see, our God is working. Our God is tilling the soil. Our God is nurturing the roots. Our God is digging out the weeds so that my dream, your dream, our dreams, can break through to the surface.

Faith for the In-Between

I felt a hand gently brush my shoulder. I turned around and met a wrinkled and anxiously smiling face I had not seen before. Worship had long been over, and I thought the church was empty. Yet, this woman had patiently waited until everyone else cleared out, and she and I were the only ones left near the sanctuary.

She asked me if I could spare a minute to answer a question about the sermon I'd just preached on Joseph's dormant dream. Then she leaned in and said in an urgent whisper, "I want you to know that I believe that. I really do. I believe that God is doing something underneath the surface and that eventually, God's vision will be made real in my life. I just, well, I just don't know what to do until then." Before I could answer, a younger woman burst into the hallway, exclaiming, "I've been looking for you everywhere, Mom! It's time to go—we've all been waiting!"

In seconds, she was whisked away, yet her question still lingered with me because I asked God the same question years earlier. I didn't wait around for a pastor after service. I was sitting in a circle of people in a fluorescent-lit conference room. This circle was a motley crew: young, old, Black, brown, white, men, and women. Yet, we had one thing that intimately connected us to one another: grief. Some of us had lost siblings, children, or spouses. Regardless of the role of the person whom we lost, we all came looking for something. Some were looking for healing, some were looking for empathy, but that evening our group leader wanted us to look for dreams.

She invited us to share a dream for the future despite our grief experience. After we all answered, I cleared my throat and said, "I believe all of those dreams will happen. I know that God is faithful. But what do we do until then?"

I had been holding on to that question for weeks. Everyone knew I was in seminary and training to be a pastor. I didn't want to be seen as faithless or doubtful. But I was desperate and willing to risk their judgment.

What do you do until then? What did I do for the days when the pain was overwhelming? What did I do on the nights when I couldn't sleep? How was I supposed to connect the dots I couldn't see, when I could still feel the crushing weight of grief?

What do I do until then?

No one answered for several minutes. I looked at the floor, and the tears began to pool behind my eyes. Maybe this was hopeless. Maybe there is no answer when dreams turn into nightmares.

But then someone broke the silence: *you look up.*

I took a deep breath. I couldn't stomach any more pithy Hallmark card grief sayings. Was this going to be followed by the mention of an angel? Or how the people we loved were now part of God's heavenly choir? But the voice continued:

You look up. When death and dreams are broken, it's easy to look down on what we lost. I spent the first two years after my daughter died in a tunnel looking down at my feet. I couldn't move. I couldn't imagine there was any life or dream worth living. But then I looked up. And I noticed all the people who were still around me. All the life that was still around me. All the dreams that were still around me. None of that changes that this part of my life wasn't where or how I dreamed it to be. But it does change what it could be. One day.

She stopped abruptly. I can't remember if anyone said anything else. But I do remember feeling like something had changed in the room. Or, maybe something had just changed within me.

I wish I could tell you that, like a flash of lightning, all of my doubts, pain, and fear went away. That when I looked up, the clouds parted, and I knew my dreams would be restored. But I'll tell you what I would have said to the whispering woman that day: what you do until then is a daily arching of the neck, a deliberate adjustment of the gaze that sometimes still hurts, but every day hurts a little less.

Until the dream comes into view, we make a daily faith choice to look up with expectation. We notice the people God has placed around us even when it's not where we want to be. We do this not because it hastens the day when the dream comes, but because it puts the dreamers standing next to us into view.

Yes, Joseph has been in a dungeon for ten long years. But God's grace is not revealed when the prison doors open, but when he looks up and sees who is dreaming next to him. Hope is not lost, and dreams are not dead when we look up and see other people. What was true for Joseph, I learned, could be true in my life and true in yours too.

He could have looked down, casting his vision on what dreams had still not come to the surface. Instead, he looks up and notices the prisoners dreaming next to him. He was assigned to attend them but was not content just to do his work and look away. He notices the people around him and asks about their pain, distress, and dreams.

Joseph's dream has not come to pass, yet he shows us what to do until then:

Look Up. There are dreamers whom God has sent to wait with us until then.

Look Up. There are dreamers God has sent us to notice and care for until then.

Look Up. There are dreams we won't ever see until we change our view.

Tell Me Your Dreams

When we look at our text, Joseph's dream looks dormant, yet God is up to something underneath the surface. It's been several years, maybe a decade, since he was put in prison. Yet, because Joseph is who he is, he's been appointed to attend to other prisoners—royal prisoners. The cupbearer and the chief baker have done something to offend Pharoah and found themselves thrown into this dungeon too.

One night, they both have dreams that disturb and confuse them. When Joseph hears of their troubling dreams, he does something that many of us struggle to do when the dots aren't connecting, or when our dreams look dormant. Joseph says, "Tell me your dreams." Joseph, whose own dream has been dormant for a decade, wants to listen to the dreams of somebody else!

Perhaps you are a fully mature, level-headed, and long-suffering Christian. If that's you, skip over the next few paragraphs. But, if that's not you (and you're like me and the other 99.9% of us), and you're still growing in your faith, then you know this scenario would be absolute torture! When the dots aren't connecting in our own lives, when our dreams look dormant, the very last thing that we want to do is listen to the dreams of somebody else.

We don't want to hear about the wedding when we're still broken from our divorce.

We don't want to hear about the baby when we're still healing from the miscarriage.

We don't want to hear about the promotion when we're still looking for a job.

We don't want to hear about the dreams being cast in someone else's life because it's a painful reminder of the unfulfilled dreams in ours. Yet, Joseph says, "tell me your dreams," because he realizes that God is not limited to fulfilling one dream at a time. Joseph says, "tell me your dreams," because God has not placed us in a zero-sum game where only one dream can win. Joseph says, "tell me your dreams," because God promises us life, and life more abundantly. Joseph says, "tell me your dreams," because, in God's economy, there is always enough. There are enough dreams to go around, and enough God to fulfill them all.

While it might feel good to tune out the dreams of others when ours are yet unrealized, it's not for our good. Joseph shows us that when we listen to the dreams of others, we awaken our spiritual memory.

When we listen to the dreams of others, we awaken our spiritual memory.

Joseph has been in prison for so long that what may have once shocked him is now mundane and expected. This reminded me of the "deepest trip" I've ever taken. While a student intern at a church in Johannesburg, South Africa, I wanted to experience everything this beautiful country had to share. I challenged one of my host families to take me somewhere to see something I could not experience anywhere else in the world. I thought maybe we'd go on a safari, climb a mountain, or sample food from the Cape. I'd soon learn that they had something else in mind. South Africa is one of the leading exporters of gold in the world, and my hosts wanted me to see what it took to bring this shiny substance to the surface. We pulled up to a decommissioned mine, strapped on helmets, and descended into the deep, dark tunnels underneath the earth. My hosts smiled encouragingly and said, "You said you wanted an experience you could get nowhere else. I think this is it!" My wide eyes may have betrayed the "gratitude" I tried to express for taking me on this unique journey.

The deeper we descended underground, the more miserable I became. My nose began to sniffle as the dust and dirt floated through the air. My eyes started to water and blink as

I tried desperately to see what was in front of me as the light became dimmer and darker.

For what seemed like an eternity, we journeyed through the mine before we began to move upward to the surface. As we approached the entrance of the mine, the tour guide advised us to close our eyes. He said it would take several minutes or longer for our eyes and body to adjust to the bright light and change in air pressure. He said something I will never forget: give your body time to recover its memory.

I think that's what happened to Joseph when he asked the cupbearer and chief baker to tell their dreams. As he listened to their words, their vivid imagery of what was to come, he began to recover his memory. His eyes began to adjust and see a God who once gave him a dream. His breathing began to calm as his heart breathed in the memory of God, who once gave him a dream. Joseph's spirit began to recover its memory.

Perhaps you are like Joseph and have been underground for a while. Maybe not literally, but spiritually you've been in a place where your dreams seem buried. In that place, it's dark, dusty, and easy to forget that God gave you a dream. God gave you a vision for your life that was distinctly different from the one you're living right now. Your eyes have adjusted to the dark place you've been. Your breathing is less deep, shallower to keep the dust of disappointment at bay. Yet, Joseph shows us there is another way.

He demonstrates that God puts other dreamers in our lives not to stir up pain and disappointment, but to stir up within us possibility and wonder. "Tell me your dream" is not just Joseph's invitation to hear the dream of the cupbearer and the chief baker. It's his invitation to himself to hear the dream that's been buried in the recesses of his heart.

Listening to the dreams of others is our invitation to recover our spiritual memory. It's our invitation to adjust our eyes again to the bright future God has for us despite the darkness of the present. It's our invitation to remember what was lost and see what is yet to be found more clearly.

Lost and Found

Ten years. Quiet.

Ten years. Not yet.

Ten years. Darkness.

Then. The. Light.

I can still feel the heaviness of the binocular straps cutting into my neck. I stood on a campground with over a dozen other ten-year-old novice astronomers desperately trying to earn our stargazing badge. Our troop leader provided us with a map of the constellations that we should identify. Each group had a little box to check if we successfully found it in the sky. We didn't have to identify every constellation, but we had to find at least one.

I looked around the campground and felt surrounded by future NASA prospects. Their worksheets were full of tick marks of the constellations they easily found. I wanted that stargazing badge to be ironed onto my vest, but I hadn't found a single constellation. I wiped the lenses of my binoculars and focused and refocused them. I squinted my eyes. I closed them and reopened them in the slim hope that in a brief moment of darkness, a star's light would be revealed.

My panic set in when our troop leader announced, "Fifteen more minutes, girls. Fill out your forms! Fifteen more minutes to earn your badges." With such a short time remaining,

I zeroed in on finding the Big Dipper. That was supposed to be the easiest and largest one to spot in the sky, but I still couldn't see it. I began to consider feigning momentary blindness as an excuse for why I had not seen a single constellation. Yet, before I could begin enacting this conspiracy, a pitying ten-year-old joined my side. She whispered something that changed everything: "Don't look for the Big Dipper, Nicole. Just look for the North Star. If you find that one star, it will help you see the big constellation. Trust me, you'll see it." I could barely make out her face in the dark, but what did I have to lose?

I stopped looking for the big constellation and focused on that one north star. Several minutes passed that seemed like several hours. But then it came into view; that one bright burning light appeared, and I finally began to see the outline of the big constellation I had been searching for.

Now, I'm not an Old Testament scholar, but I can say with absolute authority that Joseph was never a Girl Scout. If he were, I think he would've received the stargazing badge long before I did. Joseph listened to the cupbearer's and chief baker's dreams, which helped him connect the dots to God's much bigger picture for his life.

Joseph's been in prison for over a decade. He dreamed he would be a leader, but he's still a prisoner. He dreamed people would be bowing to him, but he's the one that's been doing all the bowing and scraping! His dream looked dead on the surface, but he did not allow his character to be buried with it. Instead, he held on to hope and leaned in as other dreamers shared their story. He brings bad news for the baker, but good news for Pharaoh's cupbearer. He interprets that, unlike the baker, the cupbearer will be restored to his royal position. He recognized that the imprisoned man who stood in front of him would one day soon stand in front of Pharoah—the only person with the power to free Joseph. The spark grew brighter as Joseph realized something that every dreamer must learn: sometimes the dot you need to connect God's big picture for your life is in someone else's dream.

Sometimes the dot you need to connect God's big picture for your life is in someone else's dream.

In other words, God's big picture for our lives will require us to be in relationship with one another in order to make our dreams a reality. We know that God doesn't need us or anyone else to make something happen. God speaks, and light appears; God takes a deep breath, and humanity begins to move. God takes a nap, and a rhythm of spiritual rest is established. No, God doesn't need our help to make dreams happen, but God chooses to connect our dreams to the dreams of other people. God intersects the big picture of our lives with the lives of others so that we become coproducers in God's dreams for one another.

Perhaps then, the question is not, What do I have to do to make my dream a reality? but rather, Who is God calling me to do it with? Who has God placed in my life to coproduce my dream?

Now this question seems simple, but answering it can be soul-shaking. Remember, Joseph is in prison because someone he trusted betrayed him. Someone he served faithfully turned their back on him. And before he ended up in Egypt, the family who was supposed to love and protect him instead left him for dead in a pit! Joseph has been lied to, sold, abandoned, accused, and forgotten by people he thought were coproducers of his dream, and he's not alone.

Every single person will be hurt by other people. Let me say that again. *Every single person will be hurt by other people.* It is an inevitable fact of life. Yet, that doesn't change how painful and traumatizing it can be. Especially when we experience that hurt and pain from people we put our whole trust in and love deeply. To survive this kind of trauma, we often begin a construction process. We build walls of emotional and spiritual invulnerability so that we do not open ourselves up to experiencing that kind of hurt and betrayal ever again.

Yet, in that effort to keep the pain out, we also keep out the possibility. We attempt to protect ourselves but instead miss the people God has put in our lives to coproduce our dreams. We fear being hurt in our vulnerability, but we forgo the people who help us connect the dots to God's big picture for our lives.

Joseph understands this risk, and he's willing to take it. The cupbearer may be just like his brothers. He may smile in his face now, but later, he could turn his back on him. *Or maybe not.* The cupbearer could be just like Potiphar's wife. The cupbearer could plot and deceive Joseph and when he doesn't get what he wants, accuse Joseph of a crime that lands him right back in this dungeon! *Or maybe not.* He could be like Potiphar himself, a witness to Joseph's talent, character, and leadership, and when that gets challenged, refuse to stand up for him. *Or maybe not!*

The truth is, Joseph doesn't know what this person may do in the future. He doesn't know if he will be a friend or foe. He doesn't know if he will be a coproducer of the dream God has for his life or just another person who will hurt and betray him. All Joseph knows is that it *might* be different. All Joseph is sure of is that there's a possibility this person could respond differently from the people who responded in the past. And the miracle is that after all of those disappointments, Joseph can still say "maybe."

Can you say that? Maybe? Maybe you see that the pain people caused you in the past doesn't have to dictate the behavior of the person God has placed in the present. Maybe you can take the risk because even if this person disappoints you, God will not.

Like most sermons, God asked me to live this reality before writing it. Recently, I accepted a history-making appointment at a congregation that has never called a woman or person of color as their senior pastor. As I was debating about whether this was God's call for my life, I was met with people who were extremely supportive, and people who were not so sure. I met people who had experienced great pain and disappointment as they broke stained glass ceilings, who wanted to protect me from that trauma. They warned me of how wounding it can be when people rejected their leadership because they were women or African Americans.

I prayed, I questioned, and tossed and turned for nights on end. I am not naive to the pain people inflict and the wounds they leave on our spirits. But then I remembered Joseph. I remembered that when the unknown goodness of people meets with the certain goodness of God, I can take a risk. It's not because I know that this will be easy or that these people are a part of God's dream for my life, but because I won't know unless I try. And you won't either.

Joseph's story is a reminder that the *maybe* of people pales in comparison to the *absolute yes* of God. Maybe the cupbearer will be the one to help Joseph's dream come to fruition, or maybe he won't! It doesn't really matter what the cupbearer does; it only matters what Joseph believes.

It only matters that we begin to see that God will continue to place people on our pathway, in our prisons, offices, neighborhoods—wherever we are—until we open up and connect the dots to the big expansive dream that God has for us.

So, look up, listen, and take a risk. Maybe you're right next to the north star God has sent to guide you to your dream. Maybe.

CHAPTER 4
TIMING IS EVERYTHING

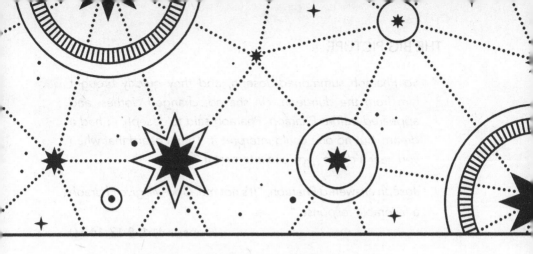

CHAPTER 4
TIMING IS EVERYTHING
Nicole

Two years later, Pharaoh dreamed that he was standing near the Nile....

In the morning, he was disturbed and summoned all of Egypt's religious experts and all of its advisors. Pharaoh described his dreams to them, but they couldn't interpret them for Pharaoh.

Then the chief wine steward spoke to Pharaoh: "Today I've just remembered my mistake. Pharaoh was angry with his servants and put me and the chief baker under arrest with the commander of the royal guard. We both dreamed one night, he and I, and each of our dreams had its own interpretation. A young Hebrew man, a servant of the commander of the royal guard, was with us. We described our dreams to him, and he interpreted our dreams for us, giving us an interpretation for each dream....

So Pharaoh summoned Joseph, and they quickly brought him from the dungeon. He shaved, changed clothes, and appeared before Pharaoh. Pharaoh said to Joseph, "I had a dream, but no one could interpret it. Then I heard that when you hear a dream, you can interpret it."

Joseph answered Pharaoh, "It's not me. God will give Pharaoh a favorable response."

(Genesis 41:1, 8-12, 14-16)

Go/No-Go

Have you heard of the term "go/no-go" before? If you have, you may be a rocket scientist or a movie buff. In space flight, "go/no-go" refers to a decision about whether to proceed at a certain juncture. When evaluating launch conditions, "go" means proceed with the launch, while "no-go" means don't launch. I first heard the term when I saw the award-winning film *Hidden Figures*. This movie illuminated the untold history of three African American female mathematicians whose work at NASA helped launch astronaut John Glenn into orbit and ultimately transformed the world. In one scene, a bespectacled Katherine Johnson is asked to determine the go/no-go point for John Glenn's reentry from orbit. This required a complicated equation to determine the exact location and timing in which Glenn would return to Earth. The math had to be just right. None of the men on staff had figured it out. Katherine stood in a room full of them, armed only with a piece of chalk and her brilliant mind.

After a few minutes of computation, Katherine confidently shared the go/no-go point. The NASA mathematicians and scientists around the table nodded their heads in awe and agreement with her calculations and moved forward with the mission. From the previous chapter, you know I could not find the Big Dipper, let alone calculate the mathematical equations that support safe reentry from rocket space explorations!

I may not understand rocket science, but I know from the life of Joseph that God operates with the same precision, timing, and intentionality. It may not always look like it or feel like it, but there is a divine design behind where we land, where we end up, and when God works in our lives. To us, it's confusing and complicated because it's all a bit over our heads. Yet we must not underestimate all of the things that God has done at exactly the right time, as well as the people God has put in our lives precisely to get us where God wants us to be.

If you think rocket science is hard, imagine what it takes to get a Jewish slave-turned-convicted-prisoner to stand before the most powerful ruler on earth in search of the exact gift he possesses in the exact time that it's needed. As we continue to connect the dots in Joseph's story, we learn that *timing is everything!*

In Genesis 40, Joseph interprets the cupbearer's dream. He tells the cupbearer that one day he will be released and restored to his royal position before Pharaoh. Joseph sees the spark of light that connects to his own dream and asks the cupbearer to remember him. He also asks the cupbearer to lift up his name or use his influence to help him. Yet, when the cupbearer is released, Joseph doesn't receive any telegram, message, or smoke signal from the cupbearer. In fact, days quickly go by, and weeks turn into months where he does not receive a single word. Scripture reveals that two years pass, and he still does not hear anything.

If you've ever waited on something, you know how long these days were for Joseph. Waiting is made all the more difficult when we can see just how close we are to our destination and yet cannot change the pace to get there any faster. This reminds me of a time when Jevon and I dared to drive into New York City from our home in Montclair, New Jersey. Our GPS said that we were only twelve miles outside of New York. In any other place in the world, a twelve-mile journey wouldn't take any time at all. However, in New York City, one of the busiest metropolises in the world, twelve miles may as well have been twelve days. We would begin to pick up speed in traffic and our hopes would lift up, and then we would screech to a halt as a truck merged into traffic and shared a signal of a flying bird to everyone who sounded their horns. We began to see New York's monuments in the sky that let us know just how close we were, but it didn't change the pace at all. We were still so far away!

Joseph knows that the cupbearer is in the palace standing next to Pharaoh, and if he would just remember Joseph, then Joseph's freedom and God's big picture for his life could finally come into view. Yet, the end of Genesis 40 ominously reveals that "the chief cupbearer did not remember Joseph, but forgot him" (Genesis 40:23 NRSV).

Joseph and every dreamer of God's dreams will have to make a decision. We have to decide whether we will trust God not only to make our dreams a reality, but to do it at just the right time. Will we surrender not only the "if" to God, but also the "when"? In other words, there's a difference between believing that God will do something and surrendering the timing to God as well.

> ### *There's a difference between believing that God will do something and surrendering the timing to God as well.*

Here's the truth: we love to proclaim the power, ability, and sovereignty of God. We sing songs about God's sovereign control over absolutely everything. We recite liturgy, calls to worship, and prayers about God's sovereign power over the earth and everything in it. Yet, we become noticeably quieter when it's time to extend God's sovereignty not only to what happens, but to when it happens.

Scriptures on waiting aren't as popular. No singers or choirs are belting out "I love to wait on God's timing!" Or "The joy I feel when I don't know when God will move." Waiting on God's sovereign timing is one of the hardest things we will ever do.

We struggle to wait because *we often interpret waiting as punishment.* If the dots are not connecting when we expected them to, we assume we have done something wrong. We conclude that God is displeased with us, and we haven't earned the dream we envision. That's why we're waiting.

If you're unsure what this looks like, book a trip to Disney World with your children, and you'll soon understand how we experience waiting as punishment. We took a trip there with our children a few years back. We spent weeks showing them the website and promotional videos so they could see all of the fun they were going to have. However, when we arrived, our children had the shock of their lives when they realized that there were two distinct lines for each attraction. One line was the general one—always the longest—full of hundreds of sweaty, hot, and dehydrated people who had been standing there for hours. The other line was the FastPass lane, always shorter with fewer sweaty and desperate-looking people. As I steered my children toward the longer line, my son finally burst out shouting, "What did we do? Why do we have to wait *here*?"

He couldn't help looking at the difference in wait times and assume that the people in the long line had done something very, very wrong! Why else would they have to wait so much longer to get to the same destination? And why else would Joseph or you and I have to wait so long to reach our dream? We look at waiting in the same manner. We imagine that God has us standing in a divine amusement park line and that those who have been "good" have received a faith FastPass, and those of us who have displeased God must join the long, hot, sweaty line of the waiting. We assume that to wait is an indication of our unworthiness to God.

When we don't interpret waiting as punishment, *we interpret waiting as wasting*. Time is a precious and limited commodity. We don't know how much of it we have, and the longer it feels like time is spent waiting for our dream to happen, the more it feels like it's wasted. Joseph hadn't seen the cupbearer for two years. I am certain that at some point, he must have wondered: Is this all just a waste of time? What is taking God so long to intervene? By the time God makes this happen, I'll be well past my prime!

After all, Joseph is approximately thirty years old now. He might have felt like he was wasting the best years of his life waiting on God—and he's not the only one who's felt this way. It's tempting for us to feel the same because wasting and waiting can look identical without context. Don't take it from me; take it from Albert Einstein.

One of the most recognizable humans on earth is the physicist Albert Einstein. Though he has been deceased for decades, his shock of white hair, large round eyes, dark suit, and occasional outstretched pink tongue are recognized around the world. His brilliance and intelligence are so well respected that his name is even used as a noun. We call people who possess superior intellectual ability "Einsteins." His impact is so universal that many of us who are not scientifically or mathematically inclined can still recite (but perhaps not explain) his most famous equation from the theory of relativity: $E = mc^2$.

Most of the pictures we see of Einstein working are at chalkboards covered in numbers or at a large mahogany desk scattered with papers. Yet, his biographers reveal that when he felt stumped or needed to think more creatively, he would leave the chalkboard and desk behind. Instead, he would pick up Lina, a violin that his mother gave him as a teenager. For several minutes or sometimes hours, he would play, play, and play. He would get lost in the violin's music and find something between those notes, strings, and his fingers that he'd take back with him to the chalkboard and desk.

If someone were to come into the room and spot Einstein serenading himself with Lina, they would assume that he was wasting precious time. Wasting and waiting can look exactly the same. Yet, Einstein would tell us that he was not wasting anything. He was simply waiting for the inspiration or the next big idea that didn't come at his desk or his chalkboard but with a violin bow in hand. It may have looked like he was wasting time, but this was time well spent.

You may not be a world-renowned physicist or a prisoner languishing in a dungeon, but the same is true for you when the dots haven't lined up, when the equation is still unsolved, when the dream is unfulfilled. It may look like you are wasting time. It may even feel like God is punishing you. Yet, God's timing is never wasteful or an act of punishment. It is always an act of grace.

God's timing is never wasteful or an act of punishment. It is always an act of grace.

Imagine this: instead of forgetting about Joseph for two years, the cupbearer went back to the palace, and on the very day he was restored, mentioned Joseph to Pharaoh. Their conversation may have gone something like this:

> *Cupbearer:* Most powerful Pharaoh, master of the universe and wearer of gold and shiny things, I am so grateful to be a cupbearer once again. While I was in prison I met a man named Joseph who helped me to interpret a dream I could not understand. He heard my dream and was able to explain that I would one day be here with you again! Perhaps you want to meet this Joseph. He was in prison because he was accused of assault, he was sold into slavery before that, and, oh, he's a Hebrew. I think you two might hit it off!

Pharaoh's response could have been any one of the following statements:

Number one: Are you talking to me? Guards! Off with his head!

Number two: You're awfully chatty. Hold the cup and keep it quiet!

Or perhaps, most realistically, number three: "What do I need with this Joseph? I've got more royal advisers, magicians, and dream interpreters than I can count. I am the most powerful ruler in the ancient Near East and I don't need some no-name imprisoned Hebrew dream interpreter! What could he possibly do for me?

It's not hard to imagine that things could have played out much differently for Joseph if the timing of the cupbearer's words to Pharaoh were shifted. When we consider it from this perspective, we recognize that God's timing is an act of grace. Joseph was waiting for two more years for the cupbearer to remember his name, and it wasn't because God was wasting time or because he was being punished. God was waiting for the time when what Joseph had to offer was exactly what was needed. God was waiting for the time when the gift that Joseph possessed would not only bless people but bring him to the place of his dreams. God was waiting for every person, place, and problem to line up so that all the dots would finally be connected. God orchestrated it all because God's timing is an act of grace.

So, what does this mean for you today? It means that God loves you and Joseph too much to connect the dots before the people and places are all lined up to make the dream happen. God has calculated the go/no-go for the big picture of your life, and God's equation of grace, love, and timing is never wrong.

Grace, Timing, and Place

We see God's timing as an act of grace because of what God is doing to orchestrate the external factors to make our dreams a reality. Yet, that's not the only reason. God's timing is also an act of grace because of what God is doing in us. Remember that when we first met Joseph, he didn't know how to handle his dreams. In fact, much of the disconnect between him and others centered around the fact that he couldn't interpret his own dreams. He couldn't make sense of them. Now he's helping other people make sense of theirs. Do you see what God has done with this time? God has taken the very thing that used to be Joseph's deficiency and made it his calling card. God has used the time that may have felt wasted to help Joseph master what used to be a shortcoming.

When Joseph's name is finally called to stand before Pharaoh, it's not his first time at bat. For the past twelve years, he's been swinging, missing, adjusting, learning, and honing his skill. In other words, when he's called to display his gift publicly, God has long been working with him privately. The reason why the years aren't wasted is not simply because of what God is doing around us, but the gift God is developing privately within us.

I've seen this not just in faraway ancient prisons, but on fairways. Over the past several months, Jevon has been learning to play golf. He has always been athletically gifted. He played football, baseball, and basketball. And though I have not asked him, he *repeatedly* shares that he still holds shooting records at Kalamazoo College, where he was a scholar-athlete.

As he approaches his forties and despite all his shooting records, his knees have formally requested a transfer to a less physically intensive sport. A friend in our congregation, Steve, offered to help Jevon take up the game of golf. Now, being the record-holding athlete that he was, Jevon imagined that they would begin with nine holes, maybe twelve before they took on a full eighteen holes of play. However, Steve, a golf coach, had very different plans.

They didn't even go to the golf course for at least six weeks. Instead, Steve took Jevon to the range where they went over the basics of golf: how to hold a club, how to place one's feet, and how to swing. Jevon didn't even have actual golf balls, but flimsy, plastic Wiffle balls to hit and hit and hit again at home. He would wind up his club, and a giant whooshing sound would rip through the air as he missed, missed, and missed another shot. As you can imagine, this created hours of laugh-out-loud, live entertainment for our entire family. And unlike our gracious God, I told Jevon I'd keep track of his records, just like Kalamazoo College did. So far, he has not broken any.

But soon, he would have the last laugh. Jevon and Steve kept practicing, and those private lessons began to pay off. The whooshing sound of missed shots was soon replaced by the loud cracks of golf balls flying across the grass. While I don't think you will catch him at the Master's Tournament anytime soon, Jevon's golf game has improved dramatically—just like my understanding of God's timing.

God works on us privately before we are called out publicly.

I've learned that Steve's golf lesson plan was a lot like the grace that God's timing gives us. God is so gracious that God hides us until we are ready. God works on us privately before we are called out publicly. God gives us the time and space to make mistakes in private. Miss shots in private. Get it wrong in private. Interpret dreams in private—when the stakes aren't so high! God gives us time to make complete fools of ourselves, to swing the club further than we do the ball, in private so that we don't make a complete fool of ourselves in public.

I can imagine that in those twelve years of waiting, Joseph didn't always get it right. Neither do we. Yet, perhaps the time we think we're wasting is really God's grace working on us privately until we're ready to be called out publicly.

If this is true, then we have to reframe the way we perceive where we are right now. If God's timing is intentional, then we are right where God wants us to be no matter where we are! Depending on where God is in our development process, it may be harder to see and say that.

When Joseph was sitting in the pit, I don't think he thought, *God, your timing is everything!* When Joseph was placed in prison, I don't think he stopped and praised God for divine timing! As Joseph waits two more years to see if the cupbearer will remember him, I am certain that he is not thanking God for just a little more time to wait! Yet, as Joseph looks back over his life, he cannot help seeing that God's timing always put him exactly where he needed to be for the next dot to connect.

Let's just go through the time line:

- **First dot:** At seventeen, Joseph has dreams that his brothers and even his parents will be bowing down to him one day. Joseph was born the eleventh of twelve sons in a Hebrew family in ancient, Near Eastern Canaan. There is no situation in the patriarchal and age-honoring culture of ancient Near Eastern Canaan where his parents and brothers will bow down to him. In this place, all ten of his older brothers would have to die before Joseph would be in a position of authority over them.

- **Second dot:** Angered by Joseph's dreams of authority, his brothers throw him into a pit and sell him into slavery in Egypt.
- **Third dot:** In Egypt, there is a different culture where Joseph might be able to lead. Joseph is in Egypt and begins to work for Potiphar. Potiphar is an official in the court of Pharaoh. Potiphar elevates Joseph because of his gifts, character, and skill. Potiphar's wife accuses Joseph of a crime he didn't commit, and he is put in prison.
- **Fourth dot:** In prison, Joseph is recognized for his abilities and put in charge of other royal prisoners. Joseph meets a cupbearer and a baker who have dreams they don't understand. Joseph interprets their dreams, and the cupbearer goes back to the palace.
- **Fifth dot:** Pharaoh has a dream that he cannot interpret, and no one else in his court can understand it either. The cupbearer remembers the person he met in prison and says to Pharaoh that he should bring him here.

What's the point? Every dot is connected not just by time but by place. Joseph doesn't become a dream interpreter in the court of Pharaoh in Canaan. That's something that can only happen in Egypt. There's no time where that dream becomes a reality in that place. Only by moving from pit to Potiphar, to prison to palace, does God's big picture for Joseph's life come into focus. So this means, that *YOU are exactly where God needs you to be.*

Staying at home with the kids.

Working in the C-suite.

Standing on the assembly line.

Healing in the hospital bed.

Starting the GED.

Taking a leave of absence.

Sitting in the therapist's office.

Kneeling at the altar.

Moving across country.

Standing at the graveside.

No matter where you are, it's right where God wants you to be. It's not just the right time. You're in the right place. Where you are is *just* the dot that God will use to connect to the next dot, and the next dot, and the next dot, until you experience the big expansive dream God has for your life. It's the right time, and you're in the right place.

How Did I Get Here?

Joseph begins to connect the dots and sees that God has put him in the right place at the right time to make his dream a reality. However, the dots didn't line up because of what Joseph has done today. The dots have lined up because of what Joseph has done in his past. This is important to recognize because we often have a fearful mentality about our past. We place a lot of emphasis on the past catching up to us in the future and having a negative impact on our lives. This idea is not without merit. The Bible has many examples of people who have made past mistakes and dealt with the consequences in the future. But sometimes, we miss the way God is connecting dots because we forget that the past can not only burden us, but bless us.

The past can not only burden us, but bless us.

Think about it. There are some things that happened in our past that we wish would never see the light of day. There are some hairstyles that we will neither confirm nor deny. There are some clothing trends that we once believed were the height of fashion, but we would not be caught dead in today! While those examples are on the lighter side, there are others from our past that aren't so easy to revisit: relationships that failed us, toxic jobs that exhausted us, mistakes that we made, or pain we inflicted on others. We may even get to a point where we disconnect some of the dots of the past because we believe there's nothing from yesterday that can bless us today.

Yet, Joseph shows us a different way of looking at the past or another way of connecting the dots. He reminds us that the past doesn't just have the power to haunt us. It has the power to bless us, too. The reason Joseph's name is mentioned to Pharaoh is not because of what he's doing presently. In fact, our scripture doesn't record that he's interpreted anyone else's dreams since the cupbearer and baker were released. Joseph's name is remembered because of something he did for someone a whole two years ago! His past comes back to bless him.

If this is true, then how we live today can create blessings that connect us to our dreams tomorrow. The trouble is that we have no idea what those things are or who those people are! So, our challenge is to treat the people and places where we find ourselves today as if they are a dot God will connect to the future dream for our lives. In other words, every person and every place *matters*.

This is hard for us to remember, especially in places or with people that we didn't imagine ourselves to be with. When we have a big vision or dream for our lives and our environment doesn't match what we dream, we can discount it instead of seeing it as a dot God will connect to something more. We can choose to withhold our best until we get to a "better" place or with "better" people.

Imagine if Joseph would have done that. Imagine if he looked at that dusty prison and decided this place is so terrible, why should I be any better? These people are inmates, so why should they matter to me? I'll save my best for when I get to the palace. I'll treat people better when I get around some better people. If Joseph would have come to the cupbearer and baker with the mindset that they didn't matter and that place wasn't worth his time, he could have missed the moment. He could have missed the singular instance where a seemingly insignificant encounter would change the trajectory of his life and move him closer to his dream.

I could have done the same thing. I was standing in a pulpit in Atlantic City, New Jersey, where fewer than thirty people were gathering in a non-air-conditioned sanctuary in July to hear me preach. I did not see the dots connecting. I had spent several years prior working in a congregation of close to two thousand members. There were ample resources for ministry, classrooms, programs, and the latest technology for connecting with congregants. In this new place and with these new people, such amenities were not available. I remember once preparing a sermon, and another pastor joked with me about how long I was spending on my message. My colleague pointed out that there would be more people at my house for Thanksgiving than there would be worshiping in the sanctuary!

Even so, I brought my best. I gave those thirty people my best, because they mattered. They mattered to God, and they mattered to me. This was where God had placed me, and I was determined to bring them the message God wanted them to hear.

Little did I know that sitting in the congregation that Sunday in July would be a woman who was visiting her family member who lived in town. This woman was the chair of a women's ministry of another church ten times our size. After the service that day, she invited me to be the keynote speaker at their upcoming retreat, where a couple hundred women would be in attendance. Part of that retreat was posted online. Several other pastors and ministry directors began to reach out and invite me to serve with their ministries. Over these last ten years since that sermon was preached for less than thirty people, I have found myself preaching in sanctuaries with thousands of worshipers, serving as the keynote speaker at international conferences, starting podcasts, and publishing books. I would not be where I am now if it wasn't for that woman who sat in the sanctuary then. It mattered how I treated those people in that place. It mattered that I gave them my best. And through it all, I didn't know who was watching! I couldn't see how God would use that place and that person to connect me to the next dot.

So, make it count. You never know what person or place from your past God will use as the reason for your name to be mentioned in the future. You never know which connection God will make months, years, or even decades later. You never know who you will need or who will need you.

So, make it count. Treat people like they matter. Treat every place like a palace. Take time for the things and people that may not "look" important. Trust that they are important, because they are. That place and those people may be the ones that finally connect the big picture.

Timing and Testimony

It was Christmas morning a few years back, and I don't know who was more excited—me, Jevon, or our three-year-old son Joshua. I had spent the last several months choosing what I thought would be the most perfect gifts for our two children: a train, a dollhouse, building blocks, and a play kitchen. Now it was time for the grand finale. I told our son to sit down, close his eyes, and not open them until I said so. On the count of three, he opened his eyes and saw a bright yellow kid-sized Corvette with a red velvet bow on the hood. He screamed with contagious joy and immediately jumped in, ready to take a ride.

Clad only in our pajamas, we breathlessly brought the car to the driveway and showed Joshua how to work the pedals. As he took off down the street, I wondered if we had done something wrong. At the pace he was going, it seemed that if he were racing a snail, the snail would win! The car moved so slowly down the pavement I was convinced we had chosen one with a broken battery.

I scooped Joshua out of the car, charged it up for a few hours, and thought, *now this is it!* He got back in the car, pressed the pedals, but it continued to move at a snail's pace. I was ready to take it back to the store and exchange it for one that was working properly, but then Jevon spotted the instruction manual I had carelessly tossed aside. It said that the little yellow corvette would never exceed three miles per hour, not because it was defective but because it was designed that way.

The car had been purposely manufactured not to exceed three miles per hour because the drivers were only three years old! The designer knew that if the car moved too fast, it would exceed the motor skills, coordination, and ability of a toddler motorist. In other words, they designed the experience based on what the driver could handle.

When we first met Joseph, he could not handle his dreams. When he dreamed of his stalk of grain standing upright and the stalks of grain belonging to his brothers bowing down to his, he ran and told them all about it! When he dreamed of the sun and moon even bowing down to him, he ran and told his father, who wondered if he would also bow down to his young son.

Many preachers and theologians have connected Joseph's retelling of his dreams to an arrogance that needed correction or punishment. But, what if it was a gift that God gave Joseph time to learn how to handle? We see in this chapter that Joseph's ability to interpret dreams has changed dramatically over the last twelve years. Rather than rush in without discretion or thought as to how his interpretation might affect the person listening, now Joseph responds differently. When the cupbearer and baker are troubled by dreams they cannot comprehend, the first words out of Joseph's mouth are, "Don't interpretations belong to God?" (40:8b). When he stands before Pharaoh, who cannot understand his dreams, Joseph tells him outright, Joseph answered Pharaoh, "It's not me. God will give Pharaoh a favorable response" (Genesis 41:16).

You see, Joseph has not spent these years being punished by God or wasting time. Rather, he's been learning how to handle his gift. His spiritual maturity has grown so much that now he's not just a dreamer, but a believer. He's not just telling people about their dreams. He wants to make sure they know who their dreams come from. Joseph has learned how to handle his gift because he's learned who gives it. He's grown in his relationship with God and as the dots continue to connect, he can handle the big picture for his life.

God's dream for your life is never just that you use your gifts, but that you grow in your faith.

Because here it is: God's dream for your life is never just that you use your gifts, but that you grow in your faith. Every gift that we are given by God, every dream that uses those gifts, points back to the dream giver. The dream is not just pointing toward a destination. It points us to a God who wants to live our dreams with us. Now, Joseph is not just a dreamer. He's a believer. And with that understanding, he's ready.

You're Ready

And just like that, all the dots connected. All the people, places, and preparation God had given Joseph led him to this moment. Pharaoh had a dream that he couldn't understand, and no one could interpret it for him. In that moment, the cupbearer finally remembered Joseph's name. He was released from the dungeon, his hair was cut, and he was given new clothes. He looked the part of a royal dream interpreter, but he may not have felt the part.

Now the time had come for the ex-convict to stand before the most powerful man in all of the Egyptian Empire. As he walked into the throne room, I'm sure his eyes had to adjust to all of the golden splendor around him. I'm sure his steps echoed as his feet moved across the polished floors. For a moment, Joseph may have wondered if he was really ready to live into his dream. Did he have what it takes? He had interpreted dreams in a prison but never in a palace! Was he really good enough? Maybe the dream that he'd hear from Pharaoh would be far more complicated than the ones he'd heard before. Was he really ready? Did all of the previous experiences, people, and places really prepare him for this?

We may never stand before Pharaoh in a palace, but we've asked these same questions. Despite God's timing and precision in connecting each dot to the big picture of our dreams, we still run into self-doubt. We wonder if we are good enough, smart enough, strong enough, attractive enough, or holy enough to live into our dream. We may be inches away from what we've spent years dreaming of, but still convince ourselves that we just aren't ready.

If that's you, stop counting all the reasons why not and just start connecting the dots. Remember how this experience taught you that. How that place allowed you to work through this. How this person showed you this and you showed them that. Connect that mistake to that lesson. Connect that challenge to that triumph. Connect that blessing to that part of your past.

You'll begin to see that God may call you out when you are unqualified, but not before you are ready. *God has been preparing you for this moment in this place, and you are ready.* You'll be able to see that between the dots nothing was an accident. God was intentional. God gave you time and space to learn how to handle your gift. God worked on you privately then so that you can now display it publicly. God used people and places from your past to bless you in the present.

You're ready. You're ready to take the next step in your faith. You're ready to lead the team. You're ready to deal with what's in front of you. You're ready for what you've been dreaming of. Not a moment too soon and not a moment too late. Because our lives are proof that God's timing is everything.

CHAPTER 5
THE MOMENT WE'VE BEEN WAITING FOR

CHAPTER 5

THE MOMENT WE'VE BEEN WAITING FOR

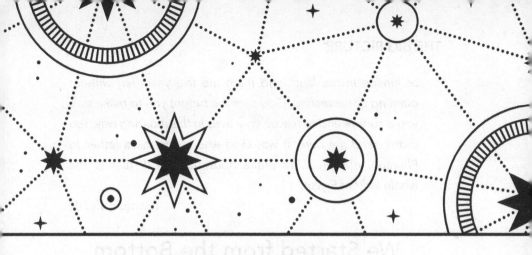

CHAPTER 5

THE MOMENT WE'VE BEEN WAITING FOR

Nicole & Jevon

Joseph could no longer control himself in front of all his attendants, so he declared, "Everyone, leave now!" So no one stayed with him when he revealed his identity to his brothers. He wept so loudly that the Egyptians and Pharaoh's household heard him. Joseph said to his brothers, "I'm Joseph! Is my father really still alive?" His brothers couldn't respond because they were terrified before him.

Joseph said to his brothers, "Come closer to me," and they moved closer. He said, "I'm your brother Joseph! The one you sold to Egypt. Now, don't be upset and don't be angry with yourselves that you sold me here. Actually, God sent me before you to save lives. We've already had two years of famine in the land, and there are five years left without planting or harvesting. God sent me before you to make sure you'd survive and to rescue your lives in this amazing way. You didn't send me here; it was God who made me a father to Pharaoh, master of his entire household, and ruler of the whole land of Egypt.

(Genesis 45:1-8)

We Started from the Bottom, Now We're Here

No one could see this coming. No one. Joseph's brothers couldn't see it. His father couldn't see it. Even Joseph couldn't predict this outcome. There was absolutely nothing in his life that hinted at Joseph being in this position. No one could foresee him becoming the governor of Egypt and overseeing the food distribution program for the entire empire. He is now second-in-command. Only Pharaoh has more power and authority than Joseph. They dressed him in their royal apparel and assigned him a royal chariot. He became popular among the people and traveled from city to city to gather and store food during the seven years of famine. He was given an Egyptian name and honored throughout the empire for his wisdom.

For the first time, it's starting to make sense. The dots are connecting. A clearer picture is beginning to unfold. One can see how God has strategically orchestrated Joseph's life to bring him to this point. Being sold to the Egyptians led him to a place where his gifts and personality could flourish. He no longer had to be relegated to a limiting and predictable future. Being falsely accused and placed in prison positioned him to be in proximity to someone who had influence with Pharaoh. When the time was right, his name was mentioned, and he stood before Pharoah not as a broken individual, but as a dreamer who has grown in his faith and wisdom.

Considering his start, Joseph's current position is quite remarkable. He began this journey as a young boy dropped into a pit, fighting for his life. By the time he's thirty, the trajectory of his life has moved in a completely different direction. If we had to guess, we might have assumed that Joseph would have remained a bitter and broken individual who relived the hurt that he experienced. It was possible, even likely, that he would grow into someone who continued the cycle of dysfunction and violence that was a part of his family history. A safe bet would have placed Joseph as a habitual offender who spent the majority of his life in and out of prison. A logical conclusion would be to label Joseph as a person sold into slavery in Egypt, who was never heard from again. Any of these stories is more predictable than where we currently find Joseph. He reminds us that it is indeed possible to go from being in a dark place to living with purpose and being used by a loving, gracious God.

This is often hard to embrace. We look at our own lives, and often convince ourselves that these two dots aren't compatible; they don't belong in the same picture. Some of the things we experience are too different, too polarizing. We began this journey by highlighting the difficulties of seeing the bigger picture when the future is unpredictable. We have a natural tendency to make judgments about the outcomes based on our starting positions. We look at the pits and perceived positions of influence and proclaim, "Those two things don't go together."

We see this incompatibility as a constant thread throughout the entire biblical story. God consistently chooses people and performs acts that are quite contradictory. God has a pattern of taking two seemingly opposing dots and experiences and making them relate. God connects barren couples to endless amounts of descendants. God connects individuals with speech impediments to leadership positions and convincing arguments about freedom. God connects a learned individual with a propensity for violence to a calling to preach the gospel.

This theme of connecting opposing dots is not limited to popular biblical stories. As pastors, we see this lived out in powerful ways. We've heard mature believers talk about growing up as atheists. We've witnessed teenage parents grow into highly respected persons in their professional fields. People raised in dysfunctional homes become the most involved caregivers. People with criminal records have enrolled in seminary. We're always amazed when we witness these connections, but no longer surprised by them.

Joseph realizes that each of his experiences was just a moment—maybe long moments, in the end, but still moments. They had a definitive beginning and a clear ending. Even the most painful and hurtful experiences he had to endure were simply moments. They lasted for a time and then passed. When the jealousy of his brothers caused him to be thrown in a pit, that was just a moment. When he was sold to an Egyptian family, it wasn't forever—just a moment. Our normal tendency is to retrieve the magnifying glass and focus the majority of our attention on one moment. Doing so gives the impression that this is the dominant image, when in reality, it's one experience out of many. It's impossible to make an accurate picture based on a single experience. The picture is far greater. That certainly was the case for Joseph. There are always more dots than we can see.

Joseph's life and those of so many others are a reminder that you can still get "there" from where you are. Embrace that small but timely affirmation "You can still get there." It's not impossible to arrive where God wants you to be from where you are currently located. Joseph's life assures us that outcomes are not fixed. It's possible for joy to come as a result of very difficult and painful experiences. It's not impossible to start in one direction and arrive at a very different and unexpected destination. So, don't allow the current experience to dictate the potential of future connections or possibilities. We are not relegated to what we are experiencing in the present. Trajectories change. People evolve. Jobs change. Circumstances are constantly changing. You can still get there.

Is This the Moment?

As Joseph initially reported to Pharaoh, after the seven years of abundance, there would be a devastating famine. It went beyond Egypt and impacted the surrounding regions as well. It spanned the empire and reached hundreds of miles away to the land of Canaan.

This was a familiar place. In these lands was an ordinary family with a rich and troubled history. This family included eleven brothers and a father who was still grieving the loss of one of his sons. The famine forced these brothers to journey to Egypt to get assistance from the one who was responsible for saving an empire.

Joseph first encounters them as just another hungry family, but this one will be different. I imagine he had done this on numerous occasions and never anticipated what would happen next. But there is a familiar scent in the air as they approach. He recognizes their walks. Their voices jog his memory. He not only remembers the people at this moment, his brothers who sold him; he remembers his dreams as well. He connects the dots.

He gets it. It makes sense. Life is lived forward but understood backward. The dream was not just a picture of Joseph in an elevated position, but it depicted others bowing at his feet. He sees it.

At one point in his life, it seemed unbelievable. Now it has become a reality. God's activity was never dependent on Joseph's full comprehension. God was working through mystery and wonder. This is the moment where we understand what we have been waiting for. It's the realization that we have what we once prayed about. There are a few things that describe such an experience. It's a feeling both of relief and amazement. It often makes us grateful for the very experiences that were the source of so many questions and skepticism.

Upon recognizing his brothers, Joseph reveals to the reader that he is indeed human. He does not let the incident pass without a response. The wise and mature Joseph exits, but the petty one takes center stage. Because they don't recognize him, Joseph pretends to be a stranger. He plays a series of mind games with them, forcing them to sit in prison and make trips to and from Canaan.

Is this the moment for which he's been waiting? Is this the moment to return the hurt that he had received? He's certainly in the position to cast judgment. What would we do or say in this situation?

Success Doesn't Heal All Wounds

Upon his brothers' arrival, we see a side of Joseph that he's not revealed to anyone. He abandons his famous stoic demeanor and cries uncontrollably. A quick read of earlier verses hints at this emotional response. When Joseph recognizes his brothers in 42:24, we find that "he stepped away from them and wept." Then again, in 43:30, when they return with their younger brother, we learn "Joseph's feelings for his brother were so strong he was about to weep, so he rushed to another room and wept there."

We see the outpouring of Joseph's emotions. We hear his anguish. It's a cry that he can no longer contain. He's tried to hold it back, but all that he's gone through over the last several years finally finds an outlet when his brothers come to buy grain. He has been waiting for a moment like this.

This moment is the first time we see Joseph express such emotion. He doesn't have a similar response when thrown into a pit. We aren't told he cries uncontrollably when he's falsely accused. He doesn't display this kind of response when he's incarcerated and forgotten for two years. The story lets us know that's he's survived his trauma, but he hasn't fully dealt with it. He doesn't know it yet, but the arrival of his brothers is a moment that he desperately needs.

Joseph reveals to us that success and even fulfilled dreams do not heal old wounds. We can't outrun every uncomfortable dot. We can't try to bury them under the accomplishments of others. The effects and impacts of certain dots linger beneath the surface of success. Something triggers those memories, and we realize that certain dots still impact us. It's hard to embrace the idea that elevation doesn't heal emotions. The dreams coming true won't solve all of our problems. It does not eliminate every struggle. It does not erase the hurt.

Recently, I saw the effects of this as I listened to the commentary around Simone Biles. She is one of the most decorated gymnasts, not just in the US but in the world. But in the 2020 Olympics, she pulled herself out of team competition because she "lost her place in the air." She admitted her fear and told those around her that it was unsafe to compete. Olympic gymnasts fly high in demanding maneuvers. A single doubt, misstep, or falter can result in injury. As people critiqued and offered their own opinions of Biles's decision, it was clear that we live in a culture that is uncomfortable with success and wounds existing simultaneously. Biles had won countless medals in professional competitions. She also grew up having to go in and out of the foster care system. She was the last competing sexual assault victim of Team USA's former national gymnastics team doctor, Larry Nasser. She was no amateur. Biles survived her pits and dominated her sport at the highest level on several occasions. The conversations about her decision to withdraw from competition revealed more about us than they did about her. We are a great audience for people to display their gifts, but not their wounds.

We've been taught to hide and bury our wounds behind success. We are afraid others will see our vulnerabilities as signs of weakness. Yet, perhaps there is a redemptive nature in our wounds. Joseph cries so loudly that the Egyptians hear it. The news reaches the house of Pharaoh.

This gives us insight into why God led Joseph to Egypt. It wasn't just a place he could dream, it was also a place where he could heal. So often, we think the next step, or the next dot, is one of increased responsibility or a climb to positional power. While that can be true, God also leads us to places where we can regroup and retreat. Egypt gave him enough distance from people who continuously tried to destroy his spirit and his dreams. He was valued more in Egypt than he was in Canaan. At home, they tore his elaborate coat, but in Egypt Pharaoh gave him another robe and a signet ring to match. He faced jealousy in the land of Canaan but was valued and embraced in Egypt. In Egypt, he was promoted, admired, and trusted. He could be, dream, and heal. For many individuals, home is a place they must escape, not where they find refuge.

These are the dots that are often underrated and undervalued. We pray more for bigger platforms than we do for wholeness. We ask God to give to us more rather than ask God to heal us. We finally get the answers to our prayers but can't embrace the moment because we are too bruised and battered. We see the bigger picture through a broken lens. This presents the danger of carrying the hurt and pain to every new place and person we experience. It's reliving the same trauma at every dot.

That is, unless we are committed to our own healing. Author Henri Nouwen uses the term "wounded healers" to describe the reality that Joseph and so many others both struggle with and embrace on a daily basis. To some extent, we are all wounded. We are wounded dreamers and wounded spouses. Wounded Parents. Wounded sons and daughters. Wounded people.

Joseph does not place the expectation for healing those wounds on the shoulders of his brothers. Even though our wounds are not always our fault, healing from them is still our responsibility. Does Joseph wait for an apology to begin the process of forgiveness? Does Joseph need closure before he starts to heal? What dots have you survived that still need to be healed?

Now I See It

With his wounds, Joseph is watching God's dream for him come true. His scars do not inhibit nor diminish God's willingness to move in his life. He is standing in front of his brothers as they bow before his feet. If the story stopped here, it would give the reader the false impression that the dream would happen just because you have it. That's what many people believe. There is hope in that. However, it gives us a false sense of God's role and responsibilities in our lives. Here's the truth that many won't admit. God is not obligated to help us fulfill our dreams.

This is not a common message, nor does it make us feel comfortable. We are often told to dream big. Let your dreams be your wings. If you can dream it, you can do it. If you work hard enough, your dreams will come true. For the majority of our lives, we are encouraged to dream.

We want to affirm and encourage the discipline of dreaming. In fact, keep dreaming. Keep thinking about a better future for yourself and generations to come. We need more people who are so dissatisfied with the current conditions that it leads them to dream.

It's important to remember, though, that this was God's dream, not Joseph's. God is the giver of the dream, and God is the one who brings it about in Joseph's life. Nowhere along this journey are we given detailed accounts or desires from Joseph. We aren't informed of what he personally wanted. At some point in Joseph's life, God's dreams simply became his dreams. He embraced the bigger picture that God had for his life and that became his starting point.

This is often different from our usual approach. Too often, we retreat to our own desires and dream apart from our connection with God. We are guided by our own thoughts and visions of the future. We compose our pictures, devise our plans, plot the course, and then ask God to bless "our" dreams. We then hold God responsible for fulfilling our dreams. We assume that's God's role. Our faith hinges on God's ability to reproduce the picture in our minds.

Joseph's story reveals one of the most important relationships that we will obtain. This relationship will determine so much of our lives. It might determine where you live. It will impact the quality of friendships. It heavily affects how we spend the limited time we have. *It is the relationship that we have with the things that we desire.*

Chasing after our dreams is not synonymous with living God's will.

If we are not careful, our dreams can become our idols. They can exist as the very distractions that keep us from fulfilling the dreams that God sees for us. It's tempting to spend more time chasing a dream than we do desiring God. The dream gets our undying devotion. We pledge our unwavering commitment. Families have been ruined from chasing dreams. We have fallen into destructive habits chasing our dreams and have missed out on meaningful moments chasing the images in our heads. Unfortunately, the most important persons in our lives have been collateral damage because of our pursuits. Life has passed us by because we were so adamant about obtaining an idea or a future that was never from God. Chasing after our dreams is not synonymous with living God's will.

The next logical question that we are challenged to ask is, "How do I know if this dream is from me or from God?" Here's how one can determine if the picture is from God or from you. Start by asking, "Is it big enough to create dependency?" A dream from God places God at the center. It won't happen, can't happen, unless God brings it about. Be careful, not every great idea is a God idea. This is not an endorsement for just going bigger with your dreams. But it is to say that dreams from God depend on a certain level of faith. If you don't need God's assistance to accomplish the dream, there is a high probability that God is not the source of it. It exists as an act of trust. It's a journey of discovering more about who we are, but most importantly, who God is. A dream from God draws us closer to God. On this journey, we witness aspects of God's character that we may not have previously embraced. Joseph does not become one of the most powerful individuals in this entire region without God's help. The dream required a level of divine participation and human dependency.

Second, a dream from God will never require you to compromise who you are. While the dream changes us, it does not ask us to become something God never intends. While Joseph was in Egypt, he never had to deny being a Hebrew or radically alter what made him unique. He brought his complete self in the house of Potiphar, to the prison, and even to the palace. He blends in and yet stands out. He lives in the delicate balance of being *in* Egypt, but not being *of* Egypt. In fact, during his tenure in Egypt, he is given an Egyptian name. He marries the daughter of an Egyptian priest. He has an Egyptian wardrobe and occupation. He is surrounded by the culture yet does not lose the essence of his own faith and culture. He is clear that God is the source of his interpretations and finds favor in every responsibility that he's given. He can be completely himself without losing the core of what makes him unique and gifted.

This does not mean that God's preferred future does not challenge who and what we are. The dream may unearth various qualities and aspects of our personalities that we never knew existed. It might reveal the "person" whom we've never encountered. However, God's dream will never ask us to shrink to the level of our surroundings or compromise our faith. It might send us to Egypt, but we must maintain our identities as children of God.

Lastly, we must ask the question, "Is this dream centered around me, or can it reach beyond me?" Initially, the dream that Joseph saw was a picture of people bowing down at his feet. It looks like a picture of "status" and positional authority. This is where most of our interpretations cease. This is the aspect of the dream that gets our attention. We focus on how this dream from God will impact us. How will it bless us? Where will it take us? While God certainly has individual plans for each of our lives, they must progress beyond self. They must evolve and grow to have a communal impact. We live in a culture that places the attention on self; God does not. God is a communal God by nature. God is concerned about people—*all people*. God is overtly interested in matters of justice, inclusion, and being in community with one another. God is specific enough to meet our individual needs but impact the lives of others. Our dreams should challenge us to think beyond ourselves. Does this dream change Joseph's life? Absolutely. However, his life changed so that he could be a blessing to others. God is using his life to impact the lives of thousands in one of the most powerful empires of this period. Now we find Joseph handing out food to starving people. *The dream wasn't just centered around Joseph's elevation. God strategically positioned him to be a blessing to others.*

Nowhere do we find Joseph being overly ambitious for any of these positions. When Joseph was in prison, he didn't apply to be warden. He didn't ask to be the governor. He did not campaign for any position. All we know is that he simply wanted to be faithful in any environment that he was given. In his faithfulness, the invitations kept coming. Opportunities found him. We aren't told his dreams; we just know that he's now living God's vision.

Saying Goodbye

Embracing God's dream for our lives will often require us to abandon our own. This might be one of the most difficult aspects of embracing God's bigger picture for our lives. It rivals the difficulties of surviving the pits and moving forward even when we have hit rock bottom. It's just as challenging as trying to navigate the relationships and purpose of an Egyptian jail cell. It will require just as much faith as standing before Pharaoh and trying to interpret his dreams. For some, this might be the most challenging decision along this journey of dreams and seeing the bigger picture. It is completely surrendering to God's will, even when it means saying goodbye to our own dreams.

Embracing God's dream for our lives will often require us to abandon our own.

We have held on to certain dreams for quite some time. Some of these visions started in our youth and stayed with us as we grew in age. We drew pictures of the future that detailed where we lived, how much we earned, what we accomplished, and the many things we would experience. These visions were accompanied with time frames and pinpoint locations. The people had been preselected. The names of the kids were already chosen. We took the liberty of making our connections between the dots. We even made several life-changing decisions based on the picture that we drafted for ourselves.

Then one day, the unthinkable happens. God either shows us something different or starts directing our lives in a particular direction. The dreams collide and come to an impasse where the two can't exist at the same time.

In our feeble attempts to outsmart the system, we try to see how much of God's will we can keep while still embracing our previous plans. How can we live in both worlds effectively? However, there can only be room for one. We arrive at a critical point where it's clear that in order to see God's bigger picture, we must say goodbye to our dreams. It hurts. It feels like the death of a family member. Remember, these are often dreams in which we have invested much of our physical and emotional energies. We have the school loans and internships to prove it. Our minds have spent countless hours imagining these dreams becoming reality. We have prayed about them on numerous occasions. They have become the definition of a fulfilled life. We have convinced ourselves that this image is the only way to find meaning and purpose.

And yet that doesn't change the reality that we must choose. If we decide to follow God's dream for our lives, we must emotionally bury the many ideas and visions we thought were destined to happen. The funeral can last for years. It's a grieving process. It's saying goodbye to the life we thought we were going to live. It's reimagining the person we thought we could become. It's letting go of the future and plans we spent years imagining. It's saying the benediction over the destinations and people we imagined. It's taking the image that we have meticulously dreamed of and courageously destroying its remains. But when we do this, what we gain outweighs what we lose. We give up our dreams, but we receive God's dreams for our lives.

Joseph didn't just abandon all dreams. He chose to make God's dreams his own. That took him places that his limited vision could not see. He was one of the younger Hebrew sons who became a person of influence in the land of Egypt. It doesn't appear this way at the funeral for our dreams, but God's dreams are always superior to our own. This is where true joy and meaning are discovered.

Truly embracing God's dream, however, is knowing that God's outcome might be different from the one we expected. This sounds simple, but it's important to articulate. The places might change. The people might be different. The process could be dramatically altered. There will be new timelines and other opportunities.

Seeing the bigger picture is not just a journey toward clarity. It's a discipline of letting go.

We never dreamed we would be on staff at St. Luke's United Methodist Church in Indianapolis, Indiana. We were previously living out our call to ministry in New Jersey. Nicole was the director of missions for the Greater New Jersey Conference, and I was pastoring at "The Mark." We spent many hours at coffee shops dreaming about doing ministry together. We let our minds wander at the many possibilities that God could do with our lives. Then we received the call from a church in Indianapolis looking for a clergy couple. It was one of the toughest decisions we would make together. It was a great opportunity, but it wasn't the picture we had drawn in those coffee shops. The people didn't look the same. The city was different. The responsibilities were not similar. We dreamed of having a shared ministry, but not like this! The hardest aspect was that by saying yes to an amazing opportunity that would bless us immensely, it meant saying no to ourselves. It was trusting that God was doing something in our lives that we couldn't see. *Seeing the big picture is not just a journey toward clarity. It's a discipline of letting go.* It's being completely open and available for God's dream, not our own, to become a reality.

Reframing: What Are You Bringing to That Moment?

How we connect the dots determines what we carry with us when the moment arrives. It's the moment for which Joseph has been waiting. He has the same individuals who threw him into a pit now groveling at his feet. Because of their actions, he's been left to die, sold into slavery, falsely accused, and thrown into prison for twelve years.

There are a variety of responses that Joseph could have displayed at that moment. Imagine the picture he could have seen or created with those dots. The picture could have been "It's your fault." "You did me wrong." What about a combination of the two? "Because this is your fault, and you did me wrong, now I'm going make you suffer a similar fate." He could have crafted a picture of abandonment. His story could have been centered on the number of individuals who failed him and never believed in him. There are many stories his dots could have told. He could have seen many pictures, and each of them would contain a certain level of accuracy. Joseph's response to his brothers' behavior brings us to a challenging question.

What story have you been telling yourself? When you reflect on the dots of your past, what picture do you see? What story or narrative has been defining you? It's the story we bring to every relationship. It's the story we bring to every place of employment. When we show up in various places, what are the stories, narratives, and defining images we carry with us? Joseph reminds us that it's possible to reframe and reconnect the various dots so that we can tell a different story—one defined by God's big picture.

As his brothers are standing before him, Joseph tells them an unexpected narrative. He reminds them, in essence, "I'm the one you sold into Egypt, but don't be so hard on yourself! Stop beating yourselves up over that. It's water under the bridge. God has positioned me so that I can save lives. [Do you hear the reframing?] Now God can use my gifts on a larger scale. We've had this famine for two years, but God has sent me ahead of you to save your lives. I'm here to help you! I thought it was just to help the people in Egypt, but now I see it was also to redeem you. What you meant for evil, God meant for good."

It's the first time Joseph has had the opportunity to tell his side of the story in such a complete and comprehensive manner. He sees it now. He connects the dots. He didn't understand the pit. He didn't understand why he was sold into slavery. He didn't understand how he could do everything right and have things still not work out. But now he sees it. He sees God's bigger picture for his life.

In Joseph's conversation with his brothers, there are very important details that he omits. Joseph does not mention being falsely accused. He does not mention anything about being incarcerated or recounting his days in prison. Those would have made for some very interesting conversations. He does not share any details about the two years in prison when he felt forgotten.

Joseph mentions more about the opportunities and blessings he's experienced over the last several years. He spends his time highlighting the good that he's been able to do and not the things that have happened to him. Joseph did not omit the former details because he had forgotten about them. I don't believe he deleted these dots from the bigger picture or filed them under the category of "don't ask, don't tell." He's not ashamed of his past. He's not so overly optimistic that he doesn't have a firm grasp on reality. That's not the case. But in that moment, Joseph made the conscious decision that those events would not dominate the narrative of his story. Those events were not the definitive images in the larger picture.

This is easier said than done. Reframing old narratives helps us to have "healed memories." It is a way of returning to old dots and reconnecting old events to help draw a different picture.

I learned the power of this practice from a retreat I attended at St. John's Downtown United Methodist Church, hosted by pastors Juanita and Rudy Rasmus. The focus of this retreat was to help men develop contemplative practices of spirituality in order to live their best lives. I need to preface my commentary about the event by expressing my previous skepticism. Contemplation had not been a major component of my spiritual journey up to that point. It was not a topic of interest, nor was it something I was excited about exploring. I have never been so wrong.

We went through a number of exercises that challenged us to reflect on our past and control our breathing. There was one particular exercise that seemed to set the tone for the remainder of our time together. The facilitator, Pastor Juanita, invited us to close our eyes and imagine a painful experience early in our lives that had been ingrained in our memories. The room went quiet, but there was a heaviness that you could feel. One by one, you could hear the emotional responses as we considered the painful dots hiding underneath the surface. We were collectively revisiting those memories that many of us have tried to delete or ones that have defined certain periods of our lives. It's what she said next that transformed the room. Pastor Juanita then invited us to imagine Jesus walking into that situation. "What do you think Jesus would say to you? What would Jesus want to tell you?"

When she asked that question, you could hear one sniffle. Then two. Then three. When we shared about the experience, most of us realized that we had been telling ourselves a narrative that was either incomplete or untrue. Many of us carried a certain image of our identity and possibilities based on these painful memories. And yet the most challenging aspect of the exercise was not just revisiting the moment but letting go of that narrative. It's hard letting go of the same story we've been telling ourselves.

A major component of these contemplative exercises centered around the practice of inviting God into those unhealed dots. Pastor Juanita asked us to rise to our feet and open our arms wide while reciting the affirmation: "I am open and willing to receive and give love." Joseph is not the only governor of Egypt, but he's a husband now. He's a father of two kids. He's a family man. This detail in the earlier chapters hints at Joseph's mindset as God's picture is slowly starting to unfold.

Joseph still sees himself worthy of receiving and giving love. He still sees himself worthy of good things. As these moments slowly start to unfold in his life, we receive small hints at how Joseph is processing all that has transpired. He had quite the past. If you met Joseph on a date and he told you about his former life, you might not give him another chance. If he was sitting across from you at a job interview and you saw a twelve-year gap on his resume, I'm sure that would raise questions. If he checked the box "yes" when asked if he had ever been convicted of a crime, most would never give him another opportunity. It would be easy for Joseph to discount himself from the blessings that God continually brings into his life. It's so tempting to talk ourselves out of the opportunities that God graciously places before us. We convince ourselves that everyone except us is deserving of good things. We can articulate every reason that should disqualify us from being on the receiving end of God's grace. It's not just his affirmation to his brothers that speaks volumes, but it's how he decided to live his best life. He decides not to relive the trauma that he experienced throughout his life. He decides to reframe the narrative of being abandoned and opens himself to receiving every opportunity God brings into his life.

Credit

Because Joseph is able to tell a different story, he is able to articulate God's continued role in his life. He has seen the hand of God connecting the various moments that seem so unrelated in the moment. As he stood before his brothers, it would have been easy to blame them for all that had occurred. They were the ones who ripped his coat and threw him into the pit. It was their idea to sell him to the traders heading to Egypt. It's only natural to assign fault when we experience pits and prisons.

Yet, Joseph sees a bigger picture even beyond their actions. It was bigger than his brothers. It went beyond Potiphar's wife. The dots were not just about the life of one seventeen-year-old but the thousands of lives of people who were starving. God did not intervene in Joseph's life just to give him a better-paying job. God did not touch the heart of Reuben or Judah to rescue Joseph so that they could have access to more. It was for Joseph to be a vessel to be a part of God's movement in the world.

Our hope as you complete this book is that as you reflect on the dots that make up your life, you see God in every moment. You rediscover the miracles that were already there. You summon the courage to tell a different story and even heal some difficult memories. For once we allow God to connect the dots, we start to see the Big Picture that is more than we could ask, think, or imagine.

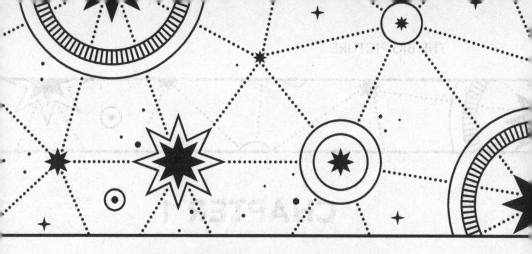

JOURNALING PROMPTS

This book asks and explores questions that are at the heart our faith journey. *Where is God in my life? What dreams does God have for me? What does this season of my life have to do with the last?*

Journaling can be a great way to reflect on your life and faith, drawing a "constellation" of faith moments, challenges, and joys as you discover God's presence in your life and unique purpose for you.

To help you navigate this faith journey, we have included a set of journaling prompts. These questions and ideas will help you chart the events of your life, identifying the dots of God's presence and grace and drawing the connections between them. Use these prompts in your own journal.

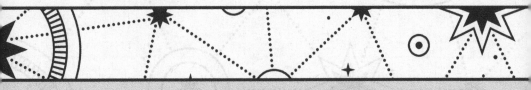

CHAPTER 1

What are your dreams? Take a moment to write your dreams. These can be small or great. List as many as you need to.

Review your list of dreams. Which one(s) feel like God's dream for your life? Why?

"Life can only be understood backwards; but it must be lived forwards." Think back across your life. What lessons have you learned in hindsight?

In what ways have you been limited by a narrow definition of what is possible? How might God be expanding your ideas about what is possible?

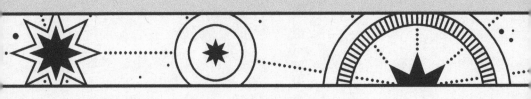

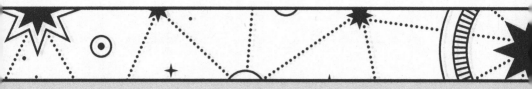

I CAN'T SEE IT

"An honest walk with God will lend you more questions than answers." What questions do your dreams raise for you?

When you struggle to make sense of your dreams, whom do you consult for guidance?

Have you had experiences where someone doubted either your abilities or ideas, or both? What impact did that have on your willingness to dream or share future ideas?

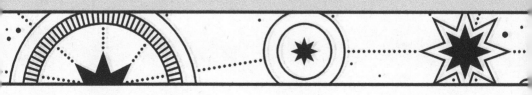

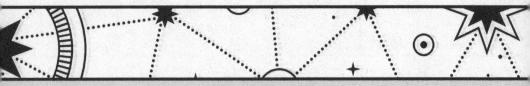

CHAPTER 2

When have you found yourself in a pit or hard place? Was it more of a private pit, public pit, or systematic one?

Reflect on your experience of the pit. How did you get there? How did you get out?

Describe a past or recent incident where you felt as though there was no way out. Where did you look for the exit doors?

What did you learn from this experience?

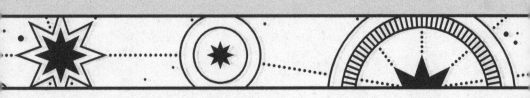

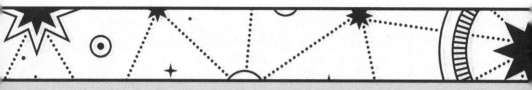

I'M A SURVIVOR

What gives you energy and spiritual nourishment in this season of your life? Where are the places where you feel most nourished?

Describe a time when you have felt or seen God's intervention in your life. How do you think the outcome would have been different if God was not present?

Personalize the phrase, "I am a _____ survivor." What have you survived? Reflect on what it means to you that you have survived this.

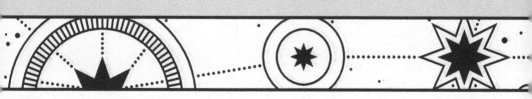

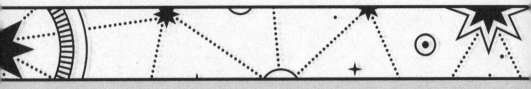

CHAPTER 3

Have there been seasons in your life when you found it difficult to dream? What was happening in your life at the time?

What dreams are dormant in your life today?

How might God be preparing you underneath the surface in this season?

What is God calling you to do in the in-between, when you are waiting on your dream?

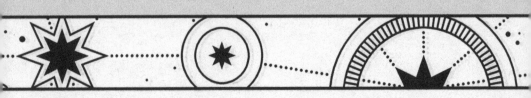

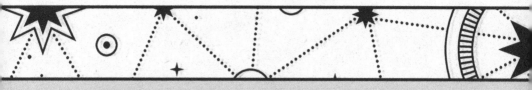

DREAMING IN PRISON

When did someone or something jog your spiritual memory?

How have you been hurt by others? Does that hurt influence your willingness to connect with others today?

Who has God placed in your life to coproduce your dream?

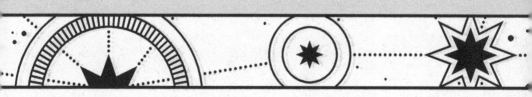

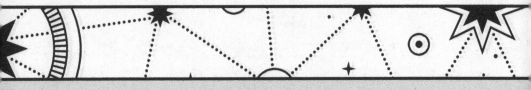

CHAPTER 4

Share a time when you later understood that waiting on God was an act of grace.

What gifts has God been developing in you privately?

How might God one day use those gifts publicly?

What experiences in your past have shown up later as blessings in your present or future? What did you do, and what do you now see that God was doing, through these experiences?

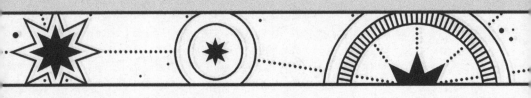

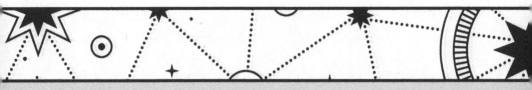

TIMING IS EVERYTHING

As you think about your dreams, what is the time-table you have for seeing them fulfilled?

How might God's timing be different from yours?

How does it feel to surrender your "when" to God?

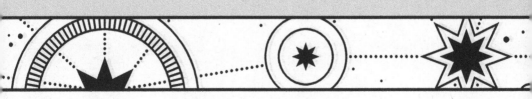

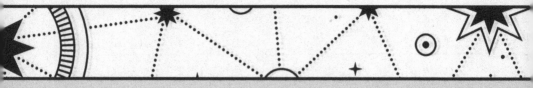

CHAPTER 5

What unhealed hurts might lie beneath the surface in your life, waiting to be dealt with?

How have you created space in your life to heal? Where and who might that space include and exclude? Where might God be calling you to take refuge and heal today?

What did you want to be when you grew up at age three, ten, or twenty-one? How did your dreams shift as you grew?

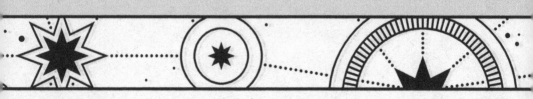

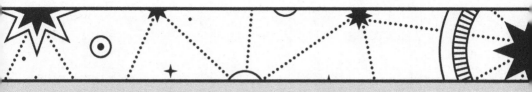

THE MOMENT WE'VE BEEN WAITING FOR

What dream do you believe God has for your life?

In what ways is God a central figure in that dream? Will achieving the dream require your trust and dependence on God?

How does the dream reach beyond you? How will it serve and bless other people?

What dreams is God calling you to say goodbye to so that you can embrace God's big picture for your life?

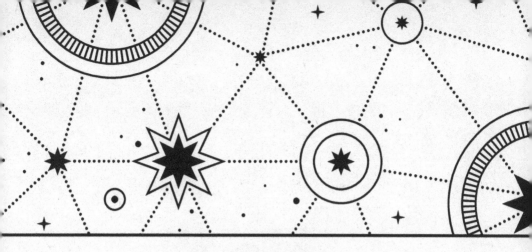

NOTES

1. Randy D. Reese and Robert Loane, *Deep Mentoring: Guiding Others on Their Leadership Journey* (Downers Grove, IL: InterVarsity Press, 2012), 32.
2. "Here's the Truth. This Is the Reality," Determined 4 Freedom, January 31, 2022, https://m.youtube.com /watch?v=soLl5vsMtKo.
3. Destiny's Child, "Survivor," by Anthony Dent, Beyoncé Knowles, and Mathew Knowles, track 1 on *Survivor*, Columbia Records, 2001.

NOTES

1. Nancy D. Reese and Robert Loban, Deep Mentoring: Guiding Others on Their Leadership Journey (Downers Grove, IL: InterVarsity Press, 2012), 22.

2. "Here's the Truth, This is the Reality," Determined A Freedom, January 31, 2022, https://temporarytube.com/watch?v=cLIbysM9Ju.

3. Destiny's Child, "Survivor," by Anthony Dent, Beyonce Knowles, and Mathew Knowles, track from Survivor, Columbia Records, 2001.

Watch videos based on *The Big Picture: Seeing God's Dream for Your Life* with Jevon and Nicole Caldwell-Gross through Amplify Media.

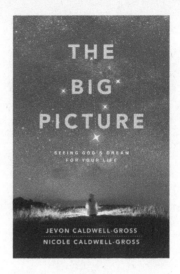

Amplify Media is a multimedia platform that delivers high quality, searchable content with an emphasis on Wesleyan perspectives for churchwide, group, or individual use on any device at any time. In a world of sometimes overwhelming choices, Amplify gives church leaders and congregants media capabilities that are contemporary, relevant, effective and, most importantly, affordable and sustainable.

With **Amplify Media** church leaders can:

- Provide a reliable source of Christian content through a Wesleyan lens for teaching, training, and inspiration in a customizable library
- Deliver their own preaching and worship content in a way the congregation knows and appreciates
- Build the church's capacity to innovate with engaging content and accessible technology
- Equip the congregation to better understand the Bible and its application
- Deepen discipleship beyond the church walls

Ask your group leader or pastor about Amplify Media and sign up today at www.AmplifyMedia.com.